Boustany

SAMI TAMIMI

Boustany

A celebration of vegetables
from my Palestine

TEN SPEED PRESS
California | New York

contents

Welcome to *Boustany*, "my garden" in Arabic

This is a book I have been, unintentionally, writing for the last four years, starting just after the publication of my last book, *Falastin*.

In the spring of 2020, my partner and I decided to take a break from the chaos of London. We packed up our house, loaded our two dogs into the car and drove all the way to our place in Umbria, Italy. What was intended to be a brief escape turned into an almost year-long stay, impacted by COVID-19. During this time, I went through a period of self-reflection and a mini-meltdown, marking a pivotal moment in my career after spending two decades managing the operations side of the Ottolenghi food and kitchens business.

While in Umbria, I cooked to soothe myself, pondering the idea of *Boustany*. The tranquility of the Italian countryside provided the perfect backdrop for introspection and culinary experimentation. Cooking was my therapy—a way to navigate my thoughts and emotions. The concept of *Boustany* emerged during this time. It was not just about creating recipes but about weaving together the stories, memories and emotions that each dish encapsulated. The recipes I developed are a reflection of my roots.

Boustany became more than just a collection of recipes; it was a journey of self-discovery and a celebration of the connections forged through food. This book is a tribute to the beauty of culinary exploration and the profound impact it can have on our lives. It is a testament to finding solace and inspiration in the kitchen, even during the most challenging times.

This book is the culmination of a lifetime of cooking and planning, though the actual work of writing the recipes began only in recent years.

Boustany takes you on a journey that tells the story of the food of my homeland, Palestine, with a fresh approach. It provides an insight into the dishes that I go back to over and over again, their recipes and the context and stories behind them.

The Palestinian cuisine

Before 1948, Palestinian cuisine reflected the region's rich culinary heritage, showcasing a diverse array of flavors and ingredients. Since then, local food in Palestine has had a deep cultural and spiritual connection to the land and farming, manifested in its quality. Our diet almost entirely consists of organic food—or baladi, as we refer to it—fresh and grown locally.

The deep connection between the people and the land stems, at least in part, from the fact that farming has been, and still is, the main source of income for many Palestinians. Staple ingredients include olive oil, grains, legumes, dates, nuts, seeds and a wide variety of fresh fruits and vegetables.

Another source of food and income for some Palestinians has been foraging. It's influenced by Palestine's diverse landscapes, offering a variety of wild edibles. Foraging for food is an important part of the culture and cuisine, as it relies on seasonality and involves gathering wild food and medicinal items from the natural environment. It's a traditional practice deeply connected to local cuisine, with people often collecting items such as wild herbs like za'atar and sage, greens such as mallow (khobiza), chicory, purslane, gundelia (akub), dandelion and also wild fruits like carob, mulberry, cactus fruit (sabr) and hawthorn (zaerur).

This is the way I grew up eating at home. Grains and pulses were cleverly transformed into flavorsome dishes adorned with vegetables and herbs, making them plentiful and incredibly colorful.

That is the beauty of the Palestinian kitchen, my childhood kitchen: the platters of steaming maftoul topped with chunky eggplant, the plump chickpea stew or the fragrant lentil fatteh that always tastes better the next day. These are the dishes I have known, loved, cooked and shared with friends. Now, I want to share them with you.

The people of Palestine

In addition to my recipes, another way to learn more about Palestine is through its people. Conversations about Palestine can quickly become political and challenging. The daily frustrations faced by Palestinians are often hard to grasp for those who don't need to carry an ID card or require a permit to travel within their own country. For Palestinians in the West Bank, the reality of checkpoints, the separation wall and a complicated system of rules paints a grim picture.

Despite these challenges, Palestinians have demonstrated remarkable courage, striving to preserve their cultural identity, maintain their sense of community and work toward a better future amid political and social hardships. This resilience is evident in many aspects of life, from cultural preservation to everyday interactions.

Palestinians are known for their warm hospitality and strong community bonds. Family and community are highly valued, and celebrations often involve abundant, delicious food, bringing people together on festive occasions. *Boustany* is my homage to the people and the land of Palestine, my spiritual home.

Boustan, the place

My grandparents on my mother's side, Hassan and Khanum, had a beautiful two-story house in Wadi Al Tufah, a quiet area in the city of Hebron, located in the southern West Bank. Their home was surrounded by a large boustan—a garden, which was a vibrant and lush space filled with a variety of fruits and vegetables that my grandfather meticulously tended all year round.

Spending time at my grandparents' house was one of the joys of my childhood. I have fond memories of running around their vast boustan, feeling the sun's warmth on my skin and the rich soil beneath my feet. The garden was a cornucopia of fresh produce, each season bringing its own bounty of fruits and vegetables. It was always packed with life and flavors, from the crisp, juicy apples and pears in the autumn to the stone fruit and fresh, leafy greens and tomatoes in the spring and summer.

My grandfather took immense pride in his garden, and his dedication was evident in the quality and abundance of the produce he cultivated. He taught me the importance of patience and care in growing food, lessons that have stayed with me throughout my life. I vividly remember the delight of picking ripe fruits straight from the trees and the satisfaction of eating vegetables that had been harvested just moments before. Family gatherings at my grandparents' house were always a feast for the eyes and senses. My grandmother would pull out all the stops, using fresh produce from the garden and mooneh—pantry—to create wonderful meals. While she could handle all the preparation herself, my mum and aunties were always eager to lend a hand with cooking, serving and cleaning up afterwards. These moments of togetherness, bonding over plates of delicious, home-grown food, were the best way to celebrate.

The flavors and aromas of those fresh, home-grown ingredients have deeply influenced my cooking. Many of my recipes draw on these cherished memories, incorporating the same fruits and vegetables that my grandfather grew with so much love and care. When I cook, I often find myself transported back to those days in the boustan, surrounded by the vibrant colors and fragrant scents of my grandparents' garden.

Boustany, the book

The dishes I have created are not just about the food; they are a way to honor the legacy of my grandparents and the love they put into their garden. Each recipe is a tribute to the flavors of my childhood and the lessons I learned from my grandfather. Through my cooking, I aim to share the warmth and joy of those days in Wadi Al Tufah, offering dishes crafted with love and a deep appreciation for nature's bounty.

There are over 100 contemporary recipes in *Boustany*: from savory to sweet, easy to proficient, soups to stews to salads, quick snacks to one-pot dishes and day-to-day dishes to those for special occasions.

The recipes are a mixture of traditional dishes that I grew up with and that will always remind me of home, my parents and my life in Jerusalem—dishes like kubbeh, fattoush and mujadara. At the same time, I didn't feel bound by the set list of traditional Palestinian dishes. I shine a new light on some of the classics and re-create them to bring fresh, exciting dishes that I love, without steering away from my loyalty to their origins. This sense of loyalty is not just about preparing or cooking a dish but also about identity—the aspect of culture that comes through the food.

Once again, I wanted to focus on Palestinian food, not just because of where I come from. I believe that Palestinian food, tradition and culture have a lot to offer the world. They are a great testimony to resilience and a way of preserving food culture by passing it down through generations.

The responsibility of writing these recipes and stories has weighed heavily on my shoulders. I hope and wish that many of you try the recipes, read the stories and want to know more about Palestine—the place, its people, its culture and its food—this wonderful place I call home.

pantry:

pickles, dairy, condiments and spice mixes

Mooneh, a term that translates to "pantry" in Arabic, is a unique concept in Middle Eastern cuisine, particularly in Palestinian and Levantine cooking.

Mooneh involves the process of preserving seasonal goods, such as nuts, grains, pulses, fruits, vegetables and dairy. The main purpose is to be able to enjoy these throughout the year, especially when they are out of season. This process is typically done by drying, pickling or otherwise preserving fruits and vegetables in a way that allows them to be stored for an extended period.

Common items that are part of mooneh include olives, pickled vegetables, sun-dried tomatoes and various types of dried herbs, jams and preserves.

Mooneh plays a significant role in maintaining the region's cultural tradition, which is passed down through generations.

PICKLES

Quick makdous (preserved eggplant in olive oil)	18
Easy pickled baby eggplant	21
Pickled fresh za'atar, chile & lemon	22

DAIRY

Labneh	23

CONDIMENTS

Burnt chile salsa	24
Shatta (red or green chile sauce)	26
Green lemon sauce	28
Red pepper paste	29
Tahini sauce	32
Sumac onions	33
Toasted nuts & seeds	35

SPICE MIXES

Gazan dukkah	36
Sweet baharat	38
Baharat	39

Preserves and pickles are a huge part of the Palestinian repertoire; they add a burst of flavor to any meal and allow seasonal vegetables to be eaten year-round. Once made, using pickles does not require planning, which is what makes mooneh (a pantry) a joy all through the year. Use these pickles to make my crushed butter beans with orange, makdous & mint (page 79).

Quick makdous does not refer to how much time this pickle needs to ferment to be ready. Rather, it refers to the amount of time required to prepare it. Traditionally, makdous is prepared with baby eggplants stuffed with garlic and walnuts. This recipe uses regular-size eggplants, resulting in an equally tasty flavor.

Quick makdous (preserved eggplant in olive oil)

Makdous Bitinjan

4 quarts | 4 liters water
1 tbsp granulated sugar
½ lemon
2 eggplants, stems trimmed and cut into 1-inch | 3cm chunks (1½ lbs | 700g)
1 cup | 100g walnuts, roughly chopped
2 green chiles, finely chopped (1 oz | 30g)
3 garlic cloves, crushed to a paste
1 tbsp red pepper paste (page 29)
1 tbsp shatta (page 26)
1¼ cups | 300ml olive oil
salt

Pour the water into a large saucepan and add the sugar, lemon and eggplant chunks. Place a plate on top of the eggplant, then place a bowl on top of the plate, so that the eggplant is completely submerged in the water. Bring to a boil, then cook over medium-high heat for 30 minutes, until the eggplant is soft and has started to look pale. Using a slotted spoon, lift the eggplant out into a colander and rinse under cold water to stop it cooking further. Place the colander over a large bowl. Place a plate on top of the eggplant and place a heavy object on top of that. Leave in the fridge for at least 12 hours (or overnight) for the eggplant to release water.

While the eggplant is cooking, place all the other ingredients except the oil in a medium bowl, add 2 teaspoons of salt, mix well to combine, then cover and leave in the fridge until needed.

After draining the eggplant for 12 hours or overnight, add it to the bowl containing the rest of the ingredients and mix well. Pack the mixture into a sterilized jar. Pour over the oil, seal the jar and turn it upside down. Sit it in a bowl to catch any oil that might seep out, and leave for 1 hour to make sure the eggplant is completely submerged in the oil. Turn the jar the right way up and store in a cool, dark place, such as a kitchen cupboard or pantry.

Leave for 12 days before using. It keeps for up to 3 months.

I love pickled things, as they often provide a necessary acidity to complement meals. This pickled baby eggplant can be enjoyed on its own with a drink, or as part of a spread. The beauty of this pickle is that it's quick, easy to make and can be eaten the next day. Heating the pickling liquid quickens the process.

The result is a hot, strong, sharp, aromatic, garlicky pickle in the best way possible. Start with eggplants as small as you can find: Japanese and regular-size ones can also work here.

Easy pickled baby eggplant

Makbus Bitinjan

1½ tbsp coarse sea salt
3 tbsp granulated sugar
1 cup | 230ml white vinegar
2 cups | 500ml water
10 baby eggplants (1 lb 5 oz | 600g)
2 tbsp coriander seeds
3 garlic cloves, halved
1 green chile, cut into 3 pieces

To serve
olive oil
chopped fresh cilantro

Put the sea salt, sugar, vinegar and water into a large saucepan and bring to a boil over high heat.

Keeping the stem intact, cut each eggplant into quarters—starting from the bottom of the eggplant, cut all the way up the stem, making sure not to cut into the stem itself.

Place the cut eggplants in the boiling pickling mixture along with the coriander seeds, garlic and green chile, bring to a boil again, then simmer over low heat for 8–10 minutes (depending on the size and freshness of the eggplants), until the eggplants are soft and cooked through.

Using a fork or a pair of tongs, transfer the eggplants into a 32 oz | 1-liter glass jar with a tight-fitting lid. Pour the pickling mixture over the eggplants, leaving about ½-inch | 1½cm of space at the top. Seal the jars and allow to cool slightly. Store in the fridge. The pickles are ready to eat the next day and will keep in the fridge for up to 3 weeks.

When ready to serve, arrange the eggplants in a serving bowl. Drizzle with plenty of olive oil and sprinkle over some chopped fresh cilantro.

As mentioned previously, foraging is an important part of the Palestinian culture and cuisine and foragers often draw on traditional knowledge, incorporating these finds into local dishes and adding unique flavors to the culinary tapestry of the region. Their mindful and sustainable foraging practices contribute to preserving the ecosystem.

This pickle epitomizes the essence of Palestinian culinary ingenuity, transforming foraged seasonal herbs such as za'atar into a delight meant to last all year round. With time, its flavors meld into a harmonious symphony.

If you can't get fresh za'atar, use any type of fresh oregano. This is a wonderful condiment to top any dip—it can be mixed into a salad, added to fried eggs or served with cheese.

Pickled fresh za'atar, chile & lemon

Makbus Za'atar w Laymonn

1½ cups | 30g fresh za'atar or
  oregano leaves
1 lemon (4 oz | 120g)
2 large green chiles, thinly sliced
  (¾ oz | 25g)
salt
¾ cup | 180ml olive oil

Wash and dry the za'atar or oregano leaves, then roughly chop it and put it into a medium bowl. Cut off and discard both ends of the lemon, then chop it into ¼-inch | ½cm cubes and add them to the za'atar, along with the sliced chiles and 1 tablespoon of salt. Mix well, then pack the mixture into a sterilized 10 oz | 300ml jar with a tight-fitting lid.

Pour over the olive oil and set the jar aside for 10 minutes, to allow any air bubbles to escape. Pop on the lid and leave in a cool place for at least 5 days before enjoying the pickle.

Labneh, a versatile Arabic staple, is a tangy, velvety strained yogurt that undergoes a simple process of salting and hanging to remove excess whey, resulting in an extra-creamy texture. The longer it's left to drain, the denser and firmer it becomes. It can be served as a dip or a spread, or it can be shaped into balls and stored in olive oil.

With its simplicity and longevity, homemade labneh offers a delicious taste of Palestinian tradition that's worth savoring time and time again.

Use the labneh to make beets with cumin labneh, toasted nuts & seeds & chives (page 104), cucumber & feta yogurt with dill, almonds & rose (page 118), garlic-infused broccoli & labneh dip (page 102) and the labneh & pomegranate ice cream (page 298).

Makes 20 balls, about 500g

Labneh

Labneh

1 quart | 1kg Greek yogurt
salt
olive oil

Line a deep bowl with cheesecloth or muslin and set aside.

In a separate bowl, mix the yogurt with 2 teaspoons of salt. Pour it into the cloth-lined bowl, then bring the edges of the cloth together and wrap tightly to form a bundle. Tie firmly with a piece of string. Hang the parcel over a bowl (or attach it to the handle of a tall jug so that the bundle can hang free—and drip—inside the jug) and leave in the fridge for 24–36 hours, until most of the liquid has drained and the yogurt is thick and fairly dry.

Another method is to put the bundle in a sieve placed over a bowl, with a plate or a couple of cans sitting on top—the weight speeds up the draining process.

Transfer the labneh to a sterilized airtight container or jar and pour over just enough olive oil so that the labneh is covered and sealed. If you want to make the labneh into balls, lightly oil your hands and spoon a small amount—about a heaping tablespoon | 20g—of labneh into the palm of one hand. Roll into a ball, repeat with the rest of the labneh, then transfer the balls to a cloth-lined baking sheet and chill for a couple of hours (or overnight) to firm up.

Half-fill a jar (one that is large enough to fit all the rolled labneh: about 4 inches | 10cm wide and 5 inches | 12cm high) with oil and drop in the balls. Top with more oil, if necessary—you want the balls to be completely covered with oil.

Seal the jar and store in the fridge for up to 3 months. Without the oil, labneh stays fresh for about 2 weeks.

I love my chiles, and I tend to have quite a few jars of pickled chiles, salsas and chile sauces of different origins in my fridge. I use them as condiments to have with any meal—for example, in my herby crushed pea & avocado toast (page 63), scrambled egg & burnt chile cherry tomato toast (page 60) and chilled tomato & avocado soup with burnt chile (page 140).

This salsa has a slightly smoky, sweet flavor and it can be delicious served with cheese or with dips such as hummus, or simply spread on a piece of buttered toast. It even plays a starring role in sandwich fillings, adding a punch of flavor that tantalizes the taste buds.

The charring of the garlic causes a bit of smoke, so you might want to ventilate the kitchen while making this, or do all the charring outside on your grill.

Burnt chile salsa

Shatta Mishwiyyeh

5 large red chiles (3¾ oz | 110g)
5 garlic cloves, unpeeled
 (1 oz | 27g)
5 tbsp | 75ml olive oil, plus more
 for sealing
1 tsp apple cider vinegar
heaping ¼ tsp ground cumin
½ tsp Urfa chile flakes (optional)
salt

Thread the chiles lengthwise onto a metal or water-soaked wooden skewer (i.e., from top to bottom). Depending on the length of your chiles (and your skewer!), you may need to use more than one. Place over the open flame of a gas burner, turning now and again, until all sides of the chiles are blackened and the flesh is starting to soften—about 4–5 minutes.

Remove the chiles from the skewer, place in a bowl and cover the bowl with a plate. Once the chiles are cool enough to handle, remove the skins (they should peel away quite easily) and seeds (if you like a hot salsa, leave the seeds in one of the chiles), then finely chop.

Repeat the process with the garlic cloves, turning them frequently until the skin is charred and the cloves are just starting to soften—about 3 minutes. Remove the skins, then finely chop the flesh and add it to the chiles, along with the olive oil, vinegar, cumin, Urfa chile flakes (if using) and a heaping ¼ teaspoon of salt. Stir well, then transfer the salsa to an 8 oz | 250ml lidded jar. If the mixture is not submerged, add more olive oil. Pop the lid on and store in the fridge.

The salsa will keep for up to 2 weeks in the fridge.

Shatta is a fiery condiment that originated in the Middle East and has become popular in Palestine, Syria, Jordan, Lebanon and Yemen. Traditionally, it is made by pounding fresh or dehydrated dried red or green chiles with salt, then leaving them in the sun for a few days to ferment. Afterwards, the chiles are combined with olive oil.

Shatta is a versatile sauce which I use in a few recipes throughout the book, such as my zucchini & leek ijeh (page 58), tahini, tomato & mint dip (page 92), fermented turnip tops (page 95) and roasted vegetables with lemon & za'atar (page 76). The main ingredient in shatta is chile peppers, and depending on the type of pepper used, the sauce can range from mild to super hot.

Shatta is not just any condiment. It adds spicy and slightly sweet flavors that can elevate any dish. Once you start making it, you'll soon realize its addictive nature and it might just revolutionize your culinary experience. Use it as a base for stews, soups or salad dressings. Or get creative and mix it with honey to spoon over fried eggs, fried halloumi or buttered toast. The possibilities are endless.

Shatta (red or green chile sauce)

Shatta Hamrah w Khadra

11 oz | 300g long red or green chiles, stems removed, thinly sliced (with seeds)
salt
2 tbsp apple cider vinegar
2 tbsp lemon juice
3–4 tbsp olive oil, enough to cover and seal

Place the sliced chiles in the bowl of a food processor with 1½ tablespoons of salt and blitz well to form a fine paste.

Transfer the chile paste to a sterilized 16 oz | 500ml lidded jar and mix well. Seal the jar and store in the fridge for 3 days.

On the third day, drain the chile paste in a sieve over a bowl, discard the liquid and pop the chile back into the jar. Add the vinegar and lemon juice, stir to combine, pour over the olive oil to seal and return the jar to the fridge.

Shatta keeps for up to 3 months. Give it a good stir before using and add a bit more oil to seal each time you return it to the fridge.

Every respected hummus shop in Jerusalem and other parts of Palestine has its own version of this fiery, tangy, slightly garlicky sauce, which gets spooned or drizzled over all hummus and other dishes to elevate every bite. This sauce serves as a delicious counterbalance to the rich, creamy texture of hummus, particularly during breakfast. Its infusion of flavors adds depth and a refreshing brightness to the dish, invigorating the palate with each spoonful.

Use the sauce as a condiment, generously spooning it over fried eggs, hearty soups and rich stews. Each dollop brings forth an additional layer of complexity, enhancing the overall experience. I've used it in some of my recipes—for example, my eggplant & chickpeas with green lemon sauce (page 179) and loaded sweet potatoes with black-eyed peas (page 182).

Green lemon sauce

Tatbeelet Laymonn Khadra

½ cup | 10g fresh parsley,
   finely chopped
1 green chile, finely chopped
5 tbsp | 75ml lemon juice
2 tbsp white wine vinegar
2 garlic cloves, crushed to
   a paste
salt

In a small bowl, combine the parsley, chile, lemon juice, vinegar, garlic and a heaping ¼ teaspoon of salt and serve at once. Keep the parsley separate if making ahead of time and add just before serving.

This sauce keeps for up to 3 days in the fridge.

Red pepper paste is a versatile condiment used as a base in various dishes, much like tomato paste. Often, both pepper and tomato pastes are used in Palestinian dishes, adding depth and complexity of flavor.

This paste can also be spread on flatbread or sandwiches and added to tahini for a quick dip or vegetable dressing. I've used it in my chilled tabbouleh soup (page 147), sweetcorn, bean & green cabbage soup (page 148), tomato kubbeh neyeh (page 199), couscous fritters with preserved lemon yogurt (page 223) and bulgur kubbeh (page 216).

Makes a small jar

Red pepper paste

Dips al Filfil

4–5 large red peppers
(2 lb 2 oz | 1kg)
2 tbsp olive oil, plus more
for sealing
6 large red chiles, trimmed
and roughly chopped
(4¼ oz | 120g)
1½ tsp sweet paprika
1½ tsp ground cumin
2 tbsp apple cider vinegar
salt

Preheat the oven to 450°F.

Place the peppers on a parchment-lined baking sheet and toss with 1 tablespoon of the oil. Bake for about 45 minutes, or until completely softened and charred. Transfer to a bowl, cover with a plate and set aside to cool for about 20 minutes. Once cool enough, remove and discard the skin, stems and seeds. Place the peeled peppers in a colander over a bowl and set aside for 30 minutes to drain. Discard the liquid.

Turn the oven down to 350°F.

Place the roasted peppers in a food processor, along with the chiles, the remaining tablespoon of oil, the spices, vinegar and 1 tablespoon of salt. Blitz for 2–3 minutes, until the mixture forms a smooth paste. Transfer the paste to a parchment-lined baking sheet and spread it out evenly. Bake for 1 hour, stirring a couple of times, until the paste has thickened.

Spoon the paste into a 16 oz | 500ml sterilized lidded jar and pour over enough oil to seal. Cover and cool slightly, then store in the fridge for up to 2 months. You can also portion the paste into small, sealable bags or use an ice-cube tray for easy access straight from the freezer. It's all about making your life easier in the kitchen.

Tahini sauce is a handy Middle Eastern condiment that is often referred to as tarator in Arabic. It's flavorful and takes just a few minutes to make. It should be creamy, garlicky, tangy and nutty—it makes the perfect accompaniment to many salads and sandwiches or can just be eaten on its own with fresh bread.

I have used this sauce in several of the recipes in the book: chunky eggplant m'tabbal (page 74), smoky chickpeas with cilantro tahini (page 88), roasted cauliflower with tahini & crushed tomatoes (page 135), loaded sweet potatoes with black-eyed peas (page 182), pointy cabbage & tahini bil siniyhe (page 191) and bulgur kubbeh (page 216), and honestly, there are hundreds of other ways to use it. The main ingredient is tahini paste, which is made by grinding toasted, hulled sesame seeds into a creamy, smooth spread. It's a similar process to making peanut butter. Once in paste form, it has a savory and nutty flavor.

Tahini paste should be pale in color, smooth and pourable. Try to use Palestinian or Lebanese tahini brands for the best results, and be sure to shake and stir the tahini before using to help it emulsify, as it can often separate.

Tahini sauce

Tahinia

Rounded ½ cup | 150g tahini paste
½ cup | 120ml cold water
3 tbsp lemon juice
1 small garlic clove, crushed to a paste
salt

Put the tahini into a small bowl, along with the water, lemon juice, garlic and a heaping ¼ teaspoon of salt. Use a spoon or a small whisk to mix the ingredients until they are completely combined and form a thick and pourable paste. Taste and adjust the seasoning by adding more lemon juice and salt.

Store in an airtight container or jar. The sauce will keep for up to a week in the fridge.

Always have a jar of these lip-smacking sumac onions in your fridge. They come in handy for transforming your hummus, fattoush or cheese sandwich, to top your falafel wrap or to add the needed acidity to a lentil soup or fatteh.

Sumac onions are a staple in several *Boustany* recipes, adding a unique flavor and acidity that's hard to replicate. Having a jar of these onions on hand will ensure that you're always ready to whip up a delicious Palestinian dish, such as my crushed lentils with tahini & soft-boiled eggs (page 50), eggplant & fava beans with eggs (page 53) and fried halloumi with purslane salad (page 164).

Makes a medium-size jar

Sumac onions

Basal bil Sumac

1 large red onion, cut in half, then each half thinly sliced
1½ tbsp sumac
7 tbsp / 100ml apple cider vinegar
7 tbsp / 100ml water
3 tbsp lemon juice
salt

Pack the sliced onion into a 16 oz / 400ml lidded jar. Add the sumac and set aside.

Place the vinegar, water, lemon juice and 1 tablespoon of salt in a medium bowl and whisk well until the salt has dissolved. Pour the vinegar mixture over the onions, cover the jar and give it a gentle shake.

The onions are ready to eat the next day. Store them in the fridge for up to 3 weeks.

Palestinians have an obsession with nuts. When not snacking on them, we use them in savory and sweet dishes. Many rice, pasta and fatteh dishes are adorned with buttered or toasted nuts to add an extra layer of crunch to these dishes. The nuts are often fried in ghee or butter, for both flavor and richness.

Double or triple this recipe and sprinkle the mix over salads, rice and pasta, or serve as a snack or part of a nibble selection spread. They're also used in my beets with cumin labneh, toasted nuts & seeds & chives (page 104) and ouzi phyllo parcels (page 224).

Feel free to play around with different nut varieties, or opt for a mix that includes sesame and nigella seeds for added depth and texture. With its versatility and irresistible flavor, these toasted nuts are sure to become a staple in your kitchen repertoire.

Makes a medium jar

Toasted nuts & seeds

Khaltet Mukassarat

½ cup | 50g blanched almonds
⅓ cup | 50g pine nuts
heaping ⅓ cup | 50g pumpkin seeds
⅓ cup | 50g sunflower seeds
2 tbsp olive oil
1 tsp Aleppo chile flakes (or regular chile flakes)
salt
1 tbsp sumac

Preheat the oven to 375°F.

Put the nuts and seeds into a medium bowl. Add the olive oil, chile flakes and ½ teaspoon of salt, and mix well so that the nuts and seeds are coated in the oil and spices. Spread the mixture out in a single layer on a parchment-lined baking sheet and roast for 10–12 minutes, turning them a couple of times.

Remove from the oven and sprinkle the sumac on top, then allow to cool completely before storing in a jar or airtight container.

These nuts keep for up to 2 weeks.

Gazans are renowned for their resilience, yet their rich culinary heritage often remains overlooked. Sadly, the challenges of living under occupation have led to the disappearance of several ingredients and recipes from Palestinian kitchens, depriving tables of their cultural richness. This traditional Palestinian recipe, also known as the "soil of the Gazans," for its earthy shade, is a captivating blend of roasted ingredients, meant to be savored by dipping pieces of bread into olive oil and then into the dukkah.

Traditional versions of Gazan dukkah begin by toasting powdered wheat berries over low heat. Once toasted, the wheat berries are combined with roasted and crushed brown lentils and a seed mixture. This is then generously seasoned with salt, sumac, lemon and plenty of red chile flakes, reflecting Gazan preferences for fiery flavors.

This flavorful blend can be sprinkled generously over salads, soups or freshly baked breads for an added burst of taste and texture. Use Gazan dukkah to make the feta, shaved cucumber & dukkah toast (page 64).

Gazan dukkah

Duqqa Ghazawiya

¼ cup | 50g cracked wheat
   or bulgur wheat
1 tsp cumin seeds
1 tsp coriander seeds
1 tsp caraway seeds
1 tsp dill seeds
3 tbsp sesame seeds
1 tbsp sumac
heaping ¼ tsp Aleppo chile flakes
   (or regular chile flakes)
salt

Preheat the oven to 400°F.

Spread the cracked wheat out on a baking sheet lined with parchment paper and toast for 10 minutes, stirring a couple of times, until it's golden. Set aside to cool.

Combine the cumin, coriander, caraway and dill seeds in a frying pan and dry-fry over medium heat, shaking the pan every so often, until fragrant. This should take about 5 minutes. Set aside to cool.

In the same pan, toast the sesame seeds for 5 minutes or so, again shaking the pan now and then so that they toast evenly, until golden, then transfer them into a small bowl and allow to cool.

Put the toasted spices, sumac and chile flakes into a spice or coffee grinder and blend for about 1 minute, until they are finely ground (keep an eye on them to make sure they don't turn into a paste). Remove and set aside. Put the cracked wheat into the grinder and blend for 2–3 minutes until powder-like, then combine with the spices, sesame seeds and a heaping ¼ teaspoon of salt and mix well.

Transfer to a container. This can be stored for up to 6 months in a cool, dark place.

With its warm and licorice-like aroma, baharat el ka'ak is a true delight for the senses. It's the star of many sweet baking recipes, infusing them with a unique and irresistible flavor.

Arab spice mixes or baharat are known in the West for their warm, earthy, nutty and sweet flavor, and are used in many savory dishes in the Middle East. Baharat el ka'ak can be used in making cookies, cakes and especially in dairy-based puddings and baking, such as in my cheese and jam pie (page 250).

Makes a small jar

Sweet baharat

Baharat el Ka'ak

7 tsp | 15g fennel seeds
4½ tsp | 8g anise seeds
2 tsp mastic
5½ tsp | 12g mahlab

Combine the fennel and anise seeds in a frying pan and dry-fry over medium heat for 3 minutes, or until fragrant, shaking the pan every so often. Set aside to cool.

Put the cooled seeds into a spice grinder or mortar and pestle with the mastic and mahlab, and grind well, until super-fine. Store in an airtight jar. It keeps for a couple of months.

38   Pantry: pickles, dairy, condiments and spice mixes

Baharat, meaning "spices" in Arabic, is an aromatic blend that is a staple in many Palestinian and Middle Eastern households. Each family often has its own unique version of this spice mix, typically passed down through generations. While the exact blend can vary, common ingredients include black peppercorns, coriander seeds, cardamom, nutmeg, cinnamon, cloves, cumin and allspice. Baharat adds a complex warmth and sweet depth to a variety of dishes. Although it's widely available to buy, I prefer to make my own mix.

Baharat

Baharat

1 tsp black peppercorns
1 tsp coriander seeds
5–6 cardamom pods
⅓ of a whole nutmeg, grated
1 small cinnamon stick,
   roughly chopped
½ tsp whole cloves
1½ tsp cumin seeds
1½ tsp whole allspice berries

Place all the spices in a spice grinder or a mortar and pestle and grind until a fine powder is formed. Store in an airtight jar container, where it will keep for 2 months.

breakfast and brunch

Palestinian breakfast is not just a meal—it's a treasured communal tradition, bringing together family and friends around a table laden with savory dishes. This leisurely feast sets a warm and welcoming tone for the day ahead, encouraging connection and conversation.

At the heart of the Palestinian breakfast are dishes meant for sharing, showcasing a rich tapestry of flavors and textures. Khobez and ka'ak, served alongside bowls of olive oil and za'atar for dipping, invite you to indulge in the simple pleasure of tearing into warm, fragrant bread. Hummus and ful medames add depth and protein to the spread, along with an assortment of cheeses, including creamy tangy labneh.

Freshly chopped vegetables and olives provide a burst of freshness, perfectly complementing the richness of the meal. And for those with a sweet tooth, butter and preserves, such as fig jam or apricot jam, add sweetness to balance the savory fare. No Palestinian breakfast is complete without plenty of sweetened mint or sage tea, a comforting accompaniment that soothes the senses.

As a proud Palestinian, I always choose savory dishes to kickstart my day, savoring each bite before indulging in sweet treats or pastries, such as French toast or a nourishing bowl of granola. And if the thought of preparing such an elaborate spread feels overwhelming, fear not—the beauty of Palestinian cuisine lies in its versatility. Any of the dishes featured in this chapter would be equally wonderful for lunch or supper, ensuring that the spirit of Palestinian hospitality can be enjoyed at any time of the day.

44

A few years back, during a trip to Bucerías, a quaint town nestled along Mexico's Pacific coast, I had my first experience of migas con huevos (also known as huevo con tortilla) for breakfast. This simple dish consists of crispy fried corn or flour tortilla, strips of sautéed onions, tomatoes, jalapeños and scrambled eggs. And back then, I thought this dish could easily be Palestinian because most of its components are readily available to us.

This lovely one-pan dish kickstarts your weekend in the best possible way. It's so easy to make, and again, it gives a bit of stale bread a new life, which always gets the thumbs-up from me.

Braised eggs with pita bread, tomatoes & za'atar

Beyd Makli ma' Khobez w Za'atar

2 pita breads (7 oz | 200g)
¼ cup | 60ml olive oil, plus more
    for drizzling
4 green onions, thinly sliced
    (3½ oz | 100g)
2 medium tomatoes, roughly
    chopped (10 oz | 285g)
1 green chile, seeded and
    finely chopped (¾ oz | 20g)
salt and black pepper
4 eggs
2 tsp za'atar

Using a small sharp knife, slice the pitas open to create two separate rounds. Tear them into bite-size pieces (roughly ¾ x 1¼-inches | 2 x 3cm).

Fry the pieces of pita in 3 tablespoons of the olive oil for about 5 minutes, then remove them from the pan. Add the remaining 1 tablespoon of oil to the pan, along with the green onions, tomatoes and chile, a heaping ¼ teaspoon of salt and a grind of black pepper. Cook for about 3 minutes.

Return the pitas to the pan, crack the eggs on top and sprinkle them with a good pinch of salt. Use a fork to gently swirl the egg whites a little bit, taking care not to break the yolks. Cover the pan and simmer gently for 7–8 minutes, until the egg whites are set but the yolks are still runny. Sprinkle with the za'atar and finish with a good drizzle of olive oil.

Gaza has its own variation of the famed falafel. While the recipe may vary depending on individual and family traditions, Gazan falafel often includes a mixture of chickpeas, fava beans, green chiles, green onions and coriander seeds.

Resembling the Egyptian falafel, which also goes under the name ta'ameya, Gazan falafel is commonly served with tahini sauce (page 32), fresh vegetables, shatta (page 26) and pita pockets, making it a flavorful and satisfying dish enjoyed by many. I prefer to make it with fava beans only.

Makes 20 pieces, to serve 4–6

Gazan fava bean falafel

Falafel Ghazawi

9 oz | 250g dried split fava beans
1 medium leek, thinly sliced,
   including most of the green
   part (3½ oz | 100g)
1 garlic clove, crushed to a paste
1 cup | 20g fresh parsley,
   roughly chopped
1 cup | 20g fresh cilantro, roughly
   chopped
1 tsp ground cumin
½ tsp baking powder
salt
1 tbsp white sesame seeds
1 tbsp coriander seeds, coarsely
   crushed
sunflower oil, for frying (about
   2 cups | 500ml)

To serve
tahini, tomato & mint dip
   (page 92)
bread
pickles

Wash the fava beans and place them in a large bowl, then cover with at least twice their volume of cold water. Set aside for 5 hours to soak.

Using a food processor, blitz the leek for 1 minute, until very fine. Drain the fava beans and combine them with the garlic, parsley and cilantro. Add half the fava bean mixture and 1 tablespoon of cold water to the leek in the processor and blitz for 2–3 minutes, scraping the sides of the processor if you need to, until you have a smooth paste. If the mixture is still crumbly, blitz it for another minute.

Transfer to a medium bowl and repeat with the other half of the fava bean mixture. Add to the bowl, then add the cumin, baking powder and 1 teaspoon of salt and mix well to combine.

With wet hands, shape the falafel by pressing 1 tablespoon of the mixture, about 1 oz | 30g, into the palm of one hand to form a ball, pressing to compact the mixture. Shape into a patty about 2¼ inches | 6cm in diameter and ½ inch | 1½cm thick. With your finger, make a dent in the middle of each patty—this will make them cook evenly on the inside. Place the falafel on a plate and continue with the rest of the mixture, making 20 falafels in all. Sprinkle the tops with the sesame seeds and crushed coriander seeds.

When ready to fry, fill a deep, heavy-bottomed saucepan, about 8 inches | 20cm in diameter, with enough oil so that it rises about 1¼ inches | 3cm up the side of the pan, and place over medium-high heat. To check that the oil is hot enough, add a little bit of the falafel mixture to the pan: if it sizzles at once, you'll know it's ready. Carefully lower the falafel in batches into the oil—you should be able to fit about 4 or 5 patties in the pan at once—and cook for 3 minutes, turning them halfway, until well browned and cooked through.

Use a slotted spoon to transfer the falafel to a plate lined with paper towels while you continue with the remaining batches, then serve straight away, with tahini, tomato and mint dip, bread and pickles.

Adas medames is a close sister of the traditional ful medames, in which the main ingredient is fava beans. Ful medames is commonly enjoyed as a hearty breakfast or a satisfying meal throughout the day. Using lentils here, instead of fava beans, makes the dish much lighter and more accessible, as canned lentils are a staple pantry item in many kitchens.

While the base ingredient changes, both versions are still prepared the same way, but garlic and chile are what really make the dish, while hearty cumin, fresh cilantro, tomato and tahini pile on layers of flavors. Serve it as always, with warm pita to scoop up the adas.

Serves 2 as a main,
4 as part of a spread

Crushed lentils with tahini & soft-boiled eggs

Adas Medames

2 large eggs (optional)
¼ cup | 60 ml olive oil, plus more
  to finish
3 garlic cloves, peeled and
  crushed to a paste
1 green chile, finely chopped
1 tsp ground cumin
1 x 14-oz | 400g can of beluga/
  brown lentils, drained and
  rinsed (12 oz | 330g)
3 medium tomatoes, peeled
  and cut into ½-inch | 1cm dice
  (10½ oz | 300g)
1 cup | 20g fresh cilantro leaves,
  roughly chopped, plus more
  whole leaves for serving
¼ cup | 60g tahini paste
3 tbsp lemon juice
5 tbsp | 70ml water
salt and black pepper

To serve
sumac onions (page 33)
pan-fried turmeric bread
  (page 241) or pita

Place the eggs (if using) in a small saucepan, cover with water and cook for 10 minutes from cold. Drain and set aside until cool enough to touch, then peel the eggs and cut them into halves, lengthwise.

Put the oil into a medium sauté pan and place over medium-high heat. Add the garlic, chile and cumin and cook for a minute, until fragrant. Add the lentils, 7 oz | 200g of the tomatoes and the chopped cilantro, and cook, stirring, for a couple of minutes, then add the tahini, lemon juice, water, 1¼ teaspoons of salt and a good grind of black pepper.

Turn the heat down to medium and cook gently, stirring, for about 5 minutes, or until hot and thickened. Roughly mash the lentils with a potato masher, so that some are broken and some remain whole.

Serve in individual bowls, with half an egg (2 if serving as a main), some sumac onions, the rest of the tomatoes, the whole cilantro leaves and pan-fried turmeric bread or pita. Finish with a generous drizzle of olive oil.

I always keep a couple of cans of ful (fava beans) in my pantry for those times when I crave a quick and satisfying late breakfast or lunch on the weekends. When simple butter and toast won't do the trick and I'm in need of something more substantial and savory, this is when fava beans come to the rescue.

You can substitute the eggs with feta cheese for an extra creamy and salty touch. Alternatively, the recipe works beautifully as a vegan dish without the eggs.

If fava beans aren't available, you can easily substitute them with other canned beans. Make sure to season the beans generously and serve them with fresh crusty bread or flatbread.

This is a truly filling and satisfying meal that never fails to impress.

Eggplant & fava beans with eggs

Bitinjan w Ful ma' Beyd

2 medium eggplants
  (around 1 lb 6 oz | 630g)
⅓ cup | 80ml olive oil,
  plus more to serve
salt and black pepper
1 onion, finely chopped
  (1¼ cups | 175g)
6 garlic cloves, crushed to a paste
1 small piece of ginger, peeled and
  finely grated (¾ oz | 20g)
1 green chile, finely chopped,
  seeds and all (¾ oz | 20g)
1 tsp chile flakes
1 tsp ground cumin
½ tsp ground cinnamon
1½ tsp tomato paste
2 plum tomatoes, chopped
  into ¾-inch | 2cm chunks
  (10½ oz | 300g)
1 x 14-oz | 400g can of
  diced tomatoes
1 x 14-oz | 400g can of
  fava beans, drained
1¼ cups | 300ml water
¾ cup | 15g fresh cilantro, roughly
  chopped, plus more to serve
4 large eggs
¼ cup | 30g sumac onions
  (page 33)

Preheat the oven to 450°F.

Cut the eggplants into 1½-inch | 4cm chunks and place in a large bowl. Mix well with 2½ tbsp | 40ml of the oil, ½ teaspoon of salt and a good grind of black pepper, then spread out on a large parchment-lined baking sheet. Roast for about 25 minutes, or until completely softened and lightly browned. Remove from the oven and set aside.

While the eggplant is roasting, make the sauce. Put the remaining oil into a large sauté pan and place over medium-high heat. Add the onion and cook for about 7 minutes, until softened and lightly browned. Add the garlic, ginger, green chile, chile flakes, spices and tomato paste and cook for another minute, or until fragrant. Add the chopped tomatoes, canned tomatoes, fava beans, water, 1¼ teaspoons of salt and a good grind of black pepper. Decrease the heat to medium and cook for 15 minutes, or until the sauce thickens.

Add the eggplant chunks and cook for 3 minutes more. Stir in the cilantro, then decrease the heat to medium-low. Make 4 wells in the sauce and crack an egg into each well. Use a fork to gently swirl the egg whites a little bit, taking care not to break the yolks. Simmer gently for 7–8 minutes, until the egg whites are set but the yolks are still runny. You can cover the pan with a lid for the last few minutes (to speed up the process).

Leave to settle and cool for a couple of minutes, then garnish with the sumac onions, additional cilantro, a drizzle of olive oil and a little salt on the eggs.

Carob trees have grown naturally in Palestine since ancient times, especially in the north and Upper Galilee. One of its most popular culinary uses is as dibs (carob molasses), which is used in making desserts and eaten for breakfast alongside tahini or halaweh (sesame halva).

Another very traditional use of carob is in making carob juice, a traditional drink especially popular during Ramadan. Carob trees also play a role in Palestine's agricultural landscape and ecosystem. They are valued for their ability to thrive in arid conditions and contribute to soil stabilization.

These fluffy pancakes are a great way to start your day or weekend. The beauty of this recipe lies in its simplicity. You can prepare the batter the night before and let it rest in the fridge. When you're ready to cook, just give it a good whisk and it's good to go. These pancakes are versatile, perfect for topping with your favorite fruit, such as banana, strawberries or mango, or simply with a sprinkle of lemon and sugar.

Cardamom pancakes with tahini, halva & carob

Fatayer ma' kharroub w Halaweh

2 large eggs
2 tbsp granulated sugar
7 tbsp | 100ml heavy cream
½ cup plus 2 tbsp | 150ml
  whole milk
2¼ cups | 9½ oz | 270g
  all-purpose flour
¾ tsp ground cardamom
½ tsp anise seeds
heaping ¼ tsp ground turmeric
2 tsp baking powder
salt
3 tbsp sunflower oil, plus more
  for frying
1 tbsp nigella seeds

To serve
3 tbsp | 50g tahini paste
2½ tbsp | 50g carob molasses
¼ cup | 60g plain halva, broken
  into large chunks
flaked sea salt

Put the eggs and sugar into a large bowl and whisk well for about 1 minute, until the sugar is dissolved and the mixture looks slightly aerated.

Add the cream and milk and give everything a good whisk before adding the flour, spices, baking powder, ¾ teaspoon of salt and the oil and keep whisking until smooth and no lumps remain. Cover the batter and let it rest for 10 minutes at room temperature. If making the batter ahead of time, remember to take it out of the fridge 15 minutes before you want to use it to allow it to come to room temperature.

When ready to make the pancakes, preheat the oven to 250°F. Line a baking sheet with parchment paper and place it in the oven.

Heat a 12-inch | 30cm nonstick pan over medium-high heat. Add 1 teaspoon of sunflower oil to the pan and spread it evenly using a paper towel. Spoon about 3 tablespoons of batter into one side of the pan (you should be able to cook 3 pancakes at a time). Sprinkle a small amount of nigella seeds on top of each pancake and cook for 1–2 minutes, until the pancakes start to turn golden-brown at the bottom. Using a spatula, carefully flip the pancakes and cook them on the other side for 1 minute more, remove from the pan and place them on the prepared baking sheet. Leave in the oven while you finish cooking the rest of the pancakes.

When ready to serve, divide the pancakes between 4 individual plates. Drizzle with tahini and carob molasses and scatter over the halva. Finish with a sprinkle of flaked sea salt and serve at once.

What better way to welcome the weekend than with the smell and sound of frying herb-loaded ijeh?

This is a thick, delicious frittata-like mixture of zucchini, leeks, peas, herbs and eggs. In Palestine, it's often made with finely chopped herbs and onions. I like the addition of fresh mint, dried mint and dill or fennel seeds. Good with chopped salad (page 80), shatta (page 26) and warm bread.

Zucchini & leek ijeh (Arabic frittata)

Ijehet Kousa w Kurrath

1⅔ cups | 250g frozen peas, thawed
2 zucchini (10½ oz | 300g)
1 small onion (5¼ oz | 150g)
1 large leek, finely chopped (6 oz | 175g)
⅓ cup plus 1 tbsp | 1¾ oz | 50g all-purpose flour
¾ cup | 15g fresh parsley, finely chopped
½ cup | 10g fresh mint leaves, thinly shredded
1¼ tsp dried mint
1 tsp Aleppo chile flakes (or regular chile flakes)
½ tsp ground turmeric
1 tsp dill or fennel seeds, slightly crushed
3 large eggs, lightly beaten
salt and black pepper
3 tbsp olive oil

To serve
lemon wedges
sour cream

Put the peas into a food processor and blitz for a few seconds—you want them to be slightly crushed but not mushy. Place in a large bowl and set aside.

Trim the zucchini and peel the onion, then, using the coarse side of a box grater, grate them onto a clean kitchen towel or muslin. Gather the ends of the kitchen towel and twist hard over a bowl to squeeze out as much liquid as possible. Add the grated zucchini and onion to the peas, along with the leeks, flour, herbs, spices, eggs, 1¼ teaspoons of salt and a good grind of black pepper. Mix well to form a uniform batter.

Place a large (12-inch | 28cm) shallow nonstick pan (with a lid) over medium heat and add the oil. When the oil is hot, add the ijeh mixture, smoothing it down to make an even patty. Partly cover the pan and cook for about 17 minutes over low heat, shaking the pan a few times to make sure the ijeh doesn't stick to the bottom, and running a rubber spatula around the sides, until the edges start to get golden brown. Get a large flat plate and it place over the pan.

Carefully invert the pan, plate and all, so that the ijeh ends up on the plate. Slide it back into the pan to cook uncovered for 15 minutes, until it is firm and cooked through. When ready to serve, slide the ijeh onto a serving plate, squeeze a little lemon juice over it and serve with lemon wedges and sour cream on the side.

I adore a simple egg on toast topped with savory bits. Egg toasts are brilliantly versatile, allowing you to use whatever ingredients you have available. This one is a quick way to get a very comforting meal on the table in no time. It's a dish as happily served for breakfast as it is for supper. The tomatoes can be made up to a day ahead and reheated before serving.

While this egg toast makes a swift and straightforward meal during busy weekdays, it is also elegant enough to serve to your guests.

Scrambled egg & burnt chile cherry tomato toast

Beyd bil Shatta w al Banadoura 'ala Toast

3 tbsp olive oil
14 oz | 400g cherry tomatoes
4 garlic cloves, thinly sliced
salt and black pepper
1 tbsp rose harissa
4 sourdough slices,
   about ½-inch | 1cm thick
2 tbsp | 35g butter, at room
   temperature
8 eggs
¼ cup | 60ml heavy cream
¼ cup | 50g sour cream
2 tbsp fresh chives, finely sliced
2 tbsp fresh oregano leaves
burnt chile salsa (page 24)

Put the oil into a large sauté pan over medium heat. When it's hot, add the tomatoes and cook, shaking the pan a few times, for about 3 minutes. Add the garlic and a heaping ¼ teaspoon of salt, and continue to cook for another 4 minutes, until the tomatoes are charred in places and starting to collapse. Stir in the harissa and set aside in a warm place.

Toast the bread slices on both sides and spread them generously with butter (leaving 1 tsp | 5g for later). Set aside.

In a medium bowl, whip the eggs and heavy cream and season with ½ teaspoon of salt and a good grind of black pepper.

Put the remaining 1 tsp butter in a large frying pan over medium-low heat. When the butter has melted and starts foaming, add the eggs. Cook, stirring often, until the eggs are just set. Spoon the eggs onto the buttered toast, then top with the tomatoes, a spoonful of sour cream and a scattering of herbs. Serve with a spoonful of burnt chile salsa for extra heat.

This is the ultimate solution for hectic weekdays—crispy olive oil toast made with your favorite bread and topped with a spectacular mixture of deliciousness.

Toast has become a staple in my house because of its simplicity and versatility. So next time you're in need of a quick and tasty meal, remember this simple yet satisfying dish. The topping can be prepared the night before; then it's just a matter of putting it all together. I'm sure you will get inspired by this and will love making it over and over again.

Herby crushed pea & avocado toast

Bazilla w Avokado 'ala Toast

2 cups | 300g frozen peas, thawed
4 green onions, finely sliced
¼ cup | 5g fresh cilantro leaves, roughly chopped
¼ cup | 5g fresh mint leaves, roughly chopped
3 tbsp | 45ml olive oil, plus more for drizzling
salt and black pepper
2 small ripe avocados, peeled and cut into 1¼-inch | 3cm chunks (about 7 oz | 200g)
4 sourdough slices, about ½-inch | 1cm thick
burnt chile salsa (page 24)

To serve
lime wedges

Put the peas into a food processor with half the green onions, herbs, 3 tablespoons of olive oil and a heaping ¼ teaspoon of salt and blitz for about a minute, until you have a chunky purée. Transfer the mixture to a large mixing bowl, add the avocado, ½ teaspoon of salt and a good grind of black pepper, and mix to combine.

Toast the bread slices on both sides and drizzle each with a little olive oil, then pile the pea and avocado mixture on top of each slice. Finish with a few dots of the chile salsa, the remaining green onion and a final drizzle of oil.

Serve with lime wedges.

This summery breakfast toast offers a fantastic blend of flavors and textures, perfect for a refreshing start to the day. The cool cucumber pairs beautifully with the salty tang of feta cheese, the aromatic dukkah and the fresh herbs.

It can also be enjoyed with a side of green salad for a satisfying lunch or dinner for added versatility. Alternatively, swapping the feta for labneh provides a creamy alternative, with the option to sprinkle crumbled feta on top for an extra burst of flavor.

Feta, shaved cucumber & dukkah toast

Jibnet Feta w Khiyar 'ala Toast

4 Persian or 2 regular
  cucumbers (9¾ oz | 280g)
flaked sea salt
7 oz | 200g feta cheese
⅔ cup | 130g Greek yogurt
1 tsp nigella seeds
½ tsp lemon zest
1 small garlic clove, crushed
  to a paste
salt
1 tbsp lemon juice
1½ tsp fennel seeds, finely
  crushed
olive oil
4 sourdough slices, about
  ½-inch | 1cm thick
1 tbsp Gazan dukkah (page 36)
1½ tsp sumac
20 fresh mint leaves

Using a vegetable peeler, peel the cucumbers from the top to bottom to make long, wide ribbons. Keep going until you get to the seedy center, which you can discard (or eat). Place the cucumber ribbons in a colander placed over a bowl, add 1 teaspoon of flaked sea salt and mix well. Set aside for 15 minutes for some of the liquid to drain.

Lightly mash the feta with a fork. Add the yogurt, nigella seeds, lemon zest and garlic and mix well until it's a spreadable consistency.

Put the cucumber into a medium bowl, add ⅛ teaspoon of salt, the lemon juice, fennel seeds, ½ tablespoon of olive oil and mix well.

Toast the bread slices on both sides and drizzle each with a little olive oil, then spread each slice with the feta mixture. Top with the cucumber, and sprinkle over the dukkah, sumac and a drizzle of oil. Garnish with the mint leaves.

small plates and spreads

There are no rules when it comes to being hosted by Palestinians, apart from the fact that they want you to be welcomed in their homes, be well fed and feel that you have been looked after in the best way possible.

Sharing food is more than just a meal for us. It holds significant cultural importance. It's a symbol of hospitality, generosity and community. We take pride in preparing and offering abundant meals for guests, highlighting the value of sharing and communal dining. This act of sharing food strengthens social bonds, expresses warmth and fosters a sense of unity among family, friends, and even strangers. It reflects the cultural emphasis on togetherness and the importance of hospitality in Palestinian traditions.

Smaller-size dishes play a big part when it comes to putting on a feast. These cleverly crafted dishes, often made from pantry staples and easy-to-prepare items, may be small in size, but they pack a punch in terms of flavor and variety. A typical spread might include olives, pickles, chopped salad, dips and perhaps some cucumber and mint yogurt.

Fermentation has been a culinary tradition in the Middle East since the tenth century, serving as a means of preserving ingredients from one season to the next. Among these cherished staples is kishk, a delicacy deeply embedded in the region's culinary heritage.

Kishk is one of those ingredients that is a staple in the pantry (mooneh). Its season starts in the summer, when milk production is at its best and the sun's heat is at its peak. Yogurt, cracked wheat and salt are combined and left to ferment at room temperature for a few days. The mixture is then spread over cloths and dried in the summer's sun for up to a week before the dried kishk is stored safely. It can be prepared with cow's, sheep's or goat's milk; however, nowadays, most of the kishk sold in local markets is made with cow's milk.

This recipe doesn't involve leaving the kishk in the sun to dry. Cracked wheat is soaked in milk or yogurt for almost a week, and fermentation is kept under control by adding small amounts of dairy every few days. After the cracked wheat soaks in the dairy products and fermentation reaches the right degree, the pre-final product is an edible dough called kishk akhdar or "green kishk." At this stage, the kishk can be formed into small balls and conserved in olive oil, as you'd do with labneh balls (page 23).

Green kishk (fermented yogurt & bulgur)

Kishk Akhdar

½ cup | 100g coarse whole-grain bulgur
2 cups | 500g Greek yogurt
salt
1½ tbsp | 25g labneh (page 23)
1 tsp dried mint
1 tsp dill seeds, coarsely crushed
1 tsp dried oregano
1 tsp Aleppo chile flakes (or regular chile flakes), plus more for serving

To serve
2–3 green onions, finely sliced (1¾ oz | 50g)
½ cup | 50g walnuts, toasted
olive oil

Put the bulgur into a small bowl, cover with water and set aside for 20 minutes. Drain, and put the bulgur into a medium bowl. Add the yogurt and 1 tablespoon of salt and mix well. Cover the bowl with a plate and leave at room temperature for up to 5 days, mixing it every day to ensure the wheat absorbs most of the yogurt.

After the 5 days, add the labneh and mix well; it should have the consistency of thick porridge. Mix in the herbs and chile and taste for seasoning, adding a bit more salt if needed. At this stage, you can store the kishk in a jar or airtight container in the fridge for up to 2 weeks.

Alternatively, green kishk can be stored in the freezer and thawed overnight before use, ensuring that its delightful taste and nutritional benefits remain intact.

To serve, spread the kishk on a serving plate and garnish with the green onions, walnuts, chile flakes and a good drizzle of olive oil.

What differentiates m'tabbal from baba ganoush is the addition of tahini to the burnt eggplant. This is a lovely and easy way to prepare this delicate version of m'tabbal, which works well with the meaty, smoky eggplant, the nutty tahini and the herbs.

   Serve with braised eggs with pita bread, tomatoes & za'atar (page 45) and with loads of bread.

Serves 4
as part of a spread

Chunky eggplant m'tabbal

M'tabbal Bitinjan

3 medium eggplants
   (about 1¾ lb | 800g)
1 garlic clove, crushed to a paste
1½ tbsp lemon juice
2 tbsp olive oil, plus more for the
   pan and drizzling
salt
1 recipe tahini sauce (page 32)
10 small fresh basil leaves
2 tbsp fresh oregano or za'atar
   leaves

Place a greased grill pan over high heat. Prick the eggplants in a few places with a small sharp knife, and once the pan is hot, grill them, turning them a few times, until they are well charred and completely collapsing, about 40 minutes.

Set aside to cool down slightly, and once they are cool enough to handle, carefully peel them, making sure to keep all the flesh in one piece. Place the flesh in a colander in your sink or over a bowl for at least an hour.

Once drained, cut the eggplants into large chunks, about 1¼ inches | 3cm, and place in a medium bowl. Add the garlic, lemon juice, olive oil and ½ teaspoon of salt and gently mix. Cover and leave to marinate at room temperature for at least 30 minutes.

Spoon the tahini sauce onto a flat serving plate, spreading it out into a large circle. Spoon the eggplant chunks and all their juices on top, then sprinkle with the herbs. Finally, drizzle with olive oil.

The salad keeps well in the fridge for up to 3 days. Make sure to bring it back to room temperature before serving.

Here's a vibrant and colorful way to serve vegetables. I like to serve them in the same dish they have been roasting in, right in the middle of the table alongside other dishes and condiments.

I've mixed the tahini sauce with roasted garlic to add extra flavor. It works perfectly, adding a deliciously sweet and nutty element. You can modify this recipe by using whatever veggies are in season.

Serves 6
as part of a spread

Roasted vegetables with lemon & za'atar

Khudar bil Laymonn w al Za'atar

2 small parsnips, peeled and cut into large chunks (7 oz | 200g)
1 small rutabaga, or 2 large turnips, peeled and cut into large batons (about 1 lb | 450g)
3 large carrots, peeled and cut into thick diagonal slices (12¼ oz | 350g)
2 red bell peppers, cut into thick batons (14 oz | 400g)
3 celery stalks, cut into 1½-inch | 4cm pieces (7 oz | 200g)
2 red onions, peeled and cut into wedges (10½ oz | 300g)
2 heads of garlic, cut in half horizontally
1 small green chile, chopped, optional
1 tbsp red shatta (page 26) or rose harissa
2 tbsp za'atar
¼ cup | 60ml olive oil
1 tbsp capers, rinsed and chopped
¾ cup plus 2 tbsp | 200ml vegetable stock or water
2 tbsp lemon juice
salt and black pepper

Tahini sauce
rounded ½ cup | 150g tahini
2 tbsp lemon juice
⅔ cup | 160ml cold water

To serve
½ cup | 5g fresh parsley, chopped
2 tsp sesame seeds, lightly toasted
1 tsp sumac

Preheat the oven to 400°F.

In a large bowl, combine the vegetables, garlic, chile, shatta, za'atar, olive oil, capers, stock or water, lemon juice, ¾ teaspoon of salt and a good grind of black pepper. Make sure all the vegetables are well coated with the oil and spices. Spread them out on a large parchment-lined baking sheet and roast for 45 minutes. Remove one of the heads of garlic from the sheet and leave the rest aside to cool down slightly.

To make the tahini sauce, squeeze out the soft garlic from the remaining roasted garlic half into a medium bowl. Mash with a fork, then add the tahini, lemon juice and heaping ¼ teaspoon of salt. Mix well, then slowly add the water, stirring as you go, until you have a sauce the consistency of Greek yogurt. Set aside.

Garnish the vegetables with the parsley, sesame seeds and sumac, and serve with the garlic tahini sauce on the side.

Small plates and spreads

I like to serve these crushed beans on toasted crusty bread. They are better than any beans on toast I've ever had. The creaminess of the beans, the freshness of the orange and mint and the sharpness of the makdous makes it the perfect, and the easiest, brunch dish to share with loved ones.

Crushed butter beans with orange, makdous & mint

Fasoulia beyda ma' Makdous

1 orange (7 oz | 200g)
5 tbsp | 75ml olive oil, plus
   more to finish
4 garlic cloves, crushed to
   a paste
2 x 14 oz | 400g cans or 1 x 25 oz |
   700g jar of butter beans
   (approx. 18 oz | 500g drained
   weight), drained and rinsed
2 tbsp lemon juice
3 tbsp | 50ml cold water
salt
2½ oz | 70g makdous (page 18)
¼ cup | 5g fresh mint leaves,
   roughly torn, plus more to serve

Finely zest the orange to get 1 tablespoon, then set aside. Using a sharp knife, cut off the top and bottom of the orange, and carefully slice away the peel. Cut the orange in half lengthwise and cut out the white core. Cut the flesh into ½-inch | 1½cm cubes and place them in a small bowl.

Heat the olive oil in a large sauté pan over medium heat and fry the garlic until fragrant, 1–2 minutes. Add the butter beans, orange zest, lemon juice, water and ½ teaspoon of salt. Cook, stirring occasionally, for 2–3 minutes, to allow the flavors to combine. Remove from the heat; then, using a potato masher, roughly mash the beans, keeping some texture—you don't want a smooth purée. Transfer to a shallow serving bowl or plate and allow to cool slightly.

Meanwhile, to make the salsa, add the makdous and mint leaves to the orange flesh and mix gently.

When ready to serve, spoon the salsa over the beans and finish with some extra torn mint leaves and a drizzle of olive oil.

Here's a rustic twist on the classic chopped salad. You can switch things up by adding tahini or yogurt to give it a different flavor.

Whether you call it salata mafrumeh, salata na'ameh, salata baladiye, or salata fallahi, it's the same fresh, vibrant Palestinian salad, which is a staple at every meal—breakfast, lunch or supper. It perfectly accompanies dishes like hummus, falafel, fritters or stews.

As with the Gazan version of chopped salad (page 83), you can do all your chopping a few hours ahead of time, but don't assemble the salad too far in advance. It tends to get watery if it sits around for too long.

Chopped salad for every occasion

Salata Mafrumeh

4 small Persian cucumbers,
  or 1 large regular cucumber
  (10½ oz | 300g)
10½ oz | 300g ripe plum tomatoes,
  cut into ¼-inch | ½cm dice
10–12 radishes, cut into ¼-inch |
  ½cm dice (4½ oz | 130g)
2 green chiles, seeded and
  finely chopped
about 5 green onions, finely
  sliced (2½ oz | 70g)
3 tbsp olive oil, plus more
  for drizzling
1½ cups | 30g fresh parsley,
  very finely chopped
1 large garlic clove, crushed to
  a paste
3 tbsp lemon juice
1 tsp dill seeds, slightly crushed
salt

Peel the cucumber and quarter it lengthwise. Cut into ¼-inch | ½cm dice, removing the seeds if you're using a large regular cucumber.

Place the cucumber in a large bowl, along with the rest of the ingredients and 1 teaspoon of salt. Mix well to combine, then transfer to a serving bowl or individual plates and drizzle with olive oil.

This is a Gazan version of chopped salad that also has fresh dill added to it. Just two rules: start with vegetables as ripe and sun-kissed as possible and use a knife as sharp as you can get it. It's a simple salad, but one that requires a lot of chopping.

Do all your chopping a few hours in advance, if you like (it can take a while, particularly if you are scaling up the recipe to feed a crowd), but don't assemble this too long before serving. It'll get watery if it sits around.

Ghazzawi tahini chopped salad

Salata Ghazawiya

4 small Persian cucumbers, or
  1 large regular cucumber, peeled,
  quartered lengthwise, seeds
  removed and cut into ¼-inch |
  ½cm dice (10½ oz | 300g)
10½ oz | 300g ripe tomatoes
  (either 2 large or 4 plum
  tomatoes), cut into
  ¼-inch | ½cm dice
10–12 radishes, cut into
  ¼-inch | ½cm dice (5 oz | 140g)
2 green chiles, seeded and
  finely chopped
about 5 green onions, finely sliced
  (2½ oz | 70g)
3 tbsp olive oil, plus more for
  drizzling
1½ cups | 30g fresh parsley,
  very finely chopped
¾ cup | 15g fresh dill, finely
  chopped
rounded ¼ cup | 80g tahini paste
1 tbsp sumac
1 large garlic clove, crushed to
  a paste
3 tbsp lemon juice
1½ tsp toasted dill or fennel seeds
salt

Place all the ingredients in a large bowl with 1¼ teaspoons of salt and mix well to combine, then transfer to a serving platter or individual plates and add a drizzle of olive oil.

Many countries have a version of this classic Middle Eastern dish, lubia or fasoulia bil zeit—green beans in a rich tomato and olive oil sauce.

This can be served hot or at room temperature, just with bread or as part of a spread. I personally always go for room temperature. Other green beans can be used for this recipe if flat ones are not available.

Serves 4 as a side or part of a spread

Green beans with leek & tomato

Fasoulia Khadra bil zeit

¼ cup | 60ml olive oil
3 leeks, cut into ¼-inch | ½cm
   slices (10½ oz | 300g)
salt and black pepper
1 carrot, peeled and thinly sliced
   (2½ oz | 70g)
4 large garlic cloves, thinly sliced
1 large green chile, finely
   chopped
2 tsp tomato paste
1 lb 2 oz | 500g flat or Romano
   beans, trimmed and cut into
   3-inch | 7–8cm long pieces
3 large tomatoes, cut into
   ½-inch | 1cm cubes (1 lb | 450g)
7 tbsp | 100ml water
1 tsp ground cumin

Heat the oil in a large sauté pan that has a lid. Add the leeks and a heaping ¼ teaspoon of salt, and cook over medium heat for 5 minutes, stirring constantly, until the leeks are soft but have no color.

Add the carrot, garlic and chile and cook for 2 minutes more. Stir in the tomato paste, then add the beans and cook for 3 minutes. Add the tomatoes, water, cumin, 1½ teaspoons of salt and a good grind of black pepper.

Bring to a boil, then cover and cook over low heat for 25 minutes. You should end up with a thick sauce—if not, remove the lid and let it boil over high heat for 5 minutes. Allow the beans to cool completely and serve as a side or as part of spread.

Qdameh or leblebi are believed to have come to the Middle East, North Africa and parts of Europe from Iran around the fifteenth century.

Qdameh is a favorite Middle Eastern roasted chickpea snack, which is eaten as you would eat salted nuts. As kids, we used to be able to buy them wrapped in a paper cone and snack on them on the way back from school. Somehow, these scrumptious things have gone out of fashion and are slightly harder to find nowadays.

You can serve the chickpeas on their own and have them as a healthy snack or to accompany drinks.

In a culinary twist, I sought to reimagine qdameh as deconstructed hummus, which is a simple yet elegant dish to kick off any meal or serve as a starter. Picture it: a platter filled with za'atar & anise crackers (page 246) or bread alongside a plate of these delicious roasted chickpeas.

Smoky chickpeas with cilantro tahini

Hummus Hab bil Tahinia w al Kuzbara

2 x 14-oz | 400g cans of chickpeas, drained and rinsed
4 tbsp olive oil, plus more for drizzling
½ tsp smoked paprika
½ tsp Aleppo chile flakes (or regular dried chile flakes)
½ tsp sweet paprika
¼ tsp ground cinnamon
salt
2 tbsp lemon juice
1 recipe tahini sauce (page 32)
1½ cups | 30g fresh cilantro, chopped, plus a few more leaves to garnish

Preheat the oven to 425°F.

Put the chickpeas into a medium bowl with the olive oil, spices and a heaping ¼ teaspoon of salt, and mix well. Spread the chickpea mixture on a parchment-lined baking dish and roast for 30 minutes, stirring a couple of times. Remove from the oven, sprinkle with the lemon juice, mix and leave to cool.

Place the tahini sauce and cilantro in a blender or food processor and mix for a couple of minutes, until they form a smooth paste.

When ready to serve, spread the tahini sauce on a serving plate, pile the chickpeas in the middle and garnish with a few cilantro leaves and a drizzle of olive oil.

This is something between a condiment and a salsa. It's great spooned alongside hummus, mashed butter beans or labneh.
I also tend to use it as a condiment with fried egg dishes and with goat cheese.

Serves 4 as a side or part of a spread

Tomato, arugula & walnut salad

Salatet Jarjeer w Banadoura

¼ cup | 40g walnuts
¼ cup | 60ml olive oil
3 garlic cloves, crushed to
   a paste
2½ oz | 70g sun-dried tomatoes
   in oil, finely chopped
2 tbsp capers, drained, rinsed
   and patted dry
1¼ cups | 25g arugula
½ cup | 10g fresh parsley
½ cup | 10g fresh cilantro
1 tbsp plus 1 tsp pomegranate
   molasses
heaping ¼ tsp Aleppo chile flakes
   (or regular dried chile flakes)
1 tsp lemon zest
salt and black pepper

Preheat the oven to 375°F.

Spread the walnuts on a parchment-lined baking sheet and toast in the oven for 10 minutes. Remove and set aside to cool. Once cool, chop by hand to a medium-fine texture and place in a medium bowl.

Put the olive oil and garlic into a small pan and cook over medium heat until fragrant and the garlic starts to color. Add the chopped tomatoes and capers and cook for a few seconds more, then take off the heat and set aside to cool down.

Finely chop the arugula and herbs and add to the cooled tomato mixture. Stir in the pomegranate molasses, chile flakes and lemon zest, along with a good grind of black pepper.

Taste and add a bit of salt if needed—however, the tomatoes and capers are already quite salty, so there's usually no need to add any more.

Tahini is the queen of the Palestinian table. It can be used in many different ways, whether spread inside a pita when making a sandwich, or baked with cauliflower and cabbage.

Here it can be served as a dip or a condiment that is refreshing and bursting with flavor. It can accompany many dishes or can even just be served with warm bread to scoop up all the juices. (See the basic tahini sauce recipe on page 32.)

Serves 4 as a side or
part of a spread

Tahini, tomato & mint dip

Tahinia ma' Banadoura w Na'na

2 large ripe tomatoes
 (12 oz | 350g), finely chopped
½ cup | 120g tahini paste
2 large garlic cloves, crushed
 to a paste
1 tbsp red shatta (page 26)
2 tsp lemon zest
¼ cup | 60ml lemon juice
salt
¼ cup | 5g fresh mint leaves,
 finely chopped, plus more
 to garnish
1 tsp dried mint
2 tbsp olive oil

Put the tomatoes into a medium bowl. Add the tahini, garlic, shatta, lemon zest, lemon juice and ¾ teaspoon of salt, and mix well so you have a slightly thick mixture. Add 1 tablespoon of cold water if you think it is too thick.

Fold in the mint and transfer the dip to a serving plate or bowl. Sprinkle the dried mint and extra chopped mint on top, and drizzle with the olive oil.

This is a real shortcut to a dip called huwairna, made from a plant that grows wild all over the Levant from spring through summer. It's from the same family as mustard, with a bitter and sharp taste.

Turnip tops are available at the beginning of winter, when turnips are in season and haven't been trimmed yet. Buy a big bunch when you see them. Roughly chop and lightly salt the leaves, then they can be kept in a sealed bag in the freezer.

Serve this dish on its own with a good spoonful of shatta (page 26), a drizzle of olive oil and some bread, as part of a spread or as a side. After a few days the huwairna will get a lovely, sharp flavor.

Serves 8
as part of a mezze or spread

Fermented turnip tops

Huwairna

14 oz | 400g turnip tops, leaves picked and very finely chopped
salt
2 cups | 600g Greek yogurt

To serve
shatta (page 26)
2 tbsp olive oil
½ tsp sumac (or heaping ¼ tsp chile flakes)

Place the chopped turnip tops in a large bowl and sprinkle with 1 tablespoon of salt. Using your hands, rub the salt into the leaves for about a minute, until they are wilted. Set aside for an hour, at room temperature.

Transfer the leaves to a fine sieve set over the kitchen sink. Rinse well under cold running water, to get rid of any remaining salt. While the leaves are still in the sieve, start squeezing them with your hand until very dry, and return them to the bowl.

Add the yogurt and 1 teaspoon of salt. Stir through, then transfer to a sterilized lidded jar or container. Keep in the fridge for at least 2 days before serving—it will be too salty and bitter before that. Once in the fridge, it will keep for at least a week.

When ready to serve, spread on a plate, spoon some shatta on top and drizzle with olive oil. Sprinkle with the sumac and serve.

Chard, or saleq, is one of the most popular greens in Palestine. It gets stuffed with rice, braised or made into a dip with tahini. This classic yet simple dish uses these succulent, mildly sharp leaves, which are sautéed and then topped with crispy onion. They pair beautifully with tahini sauce (page 32).

Serves 4 as a side or part of a spread

Braised chard with crispy onions & sumac

Saleq ma' Basal

1 lb | 450g Swiss chard, leaves pulled off the stems, and leaves and stems chopped into roughly ¾ inch | 2cm pieces
6 tbsp | 90ml sunflower oil
1 medium onion (6 oz | 175g), thinly sliced
1 tbsp cornstarch
3 tbsp olive oil
salt
1 small garlic clove, thinly sliced
½ tsp Aleppo chile flakes (or regular dried chile flakes)
2 tsp sumac
lemon wedges, to serve

Bring a large pan of salted water to a boil and add the chard stalks. Simmer for 2 minutes, then add the leaves and cook for a further minute. Drain and rinse well under cold water. Allow the water to drain, then use your hands to squeeze the chard well until it is completely dry.

To make the crispy onions, put the sunflower oil into a small saucepan or small high-sided frying pan and place over high heat—the oil should be about 1¼ inches | 3cm deep.

Mix the onion and cornstarch and, once the oil is hot, carefully add the onion in batches and fry for 2–3 minutes, until golden brown, then transfer to paper towels to drain and sprinkle with a little salt. Repeat in batches until all the onions are fried.

Heat the olive oil in a medium saucepan over medium heat. Once hot, add the garlic and fry gently until it starts to become golden. Add the chard and cook for 2–3 minutes, stirring occasionally, until the chard is completely warmed through. Add the chile flakes, half of the sumac and ¾ teaspoon of salt, and mix gently.

Transfer the chard to a serving dish and top with the crispy onions and the remaining sumac. Serve with lemon wedges.

Small plates and spreads

salads

In Palestinian tradition, as with other regions across the Middle East, the dining table is adorned with a rich variety of salad dishes. These salads, deeply rooted in our culture, are not just accompaniments but an essential part of the meal spread, reflecting our love for fresh and vibrant food.

We take pride in offering a selection of small and large plates, both cooked and raw vegetable-based salads, tantalizing the senses with textures, colors and flavors.

Substantial dishes, such as Sha'aktoura, Mejadara, Fattet Adas and Kubbet Hileh, are served with a simple chopped salad. It is also common to have a salad on its own with some fresh bread, which we call taghmees, roughly translating to "dipping a piece of bread" or "mopping up the salad and its juices."

In Palestine, the salad is always eaten with a couple of side condiments, such as pickles, olives and a piece of cheese, and shatta or fresh chile for that kick which we adore throughout the region.

In this chapter, I aim to dig deeper into the kingdom of all-in-one plates of food, where vegetables take center stage and become the focal point of the meal—celebrating the diverse and abundant offerings of a salad. No longer relegated to the side as mere accompaniments, salads emerge as the focal point of a meal, captivating the palate.

Join me on this journey as we celebrate the beauty of the Palestinian way into salads, from their humble beginnings as simple accompaniments to their rightful place as stars of the meal.

The story goes like this: one day, I opened my fridge and saw a lonely head of broccoli staring back at me. Craving a flavorful yet easy lunch option, I sought to create something delicious without the need for extensive cooking. Inspired by Palestinian cuisine, where cooked greens often become delicious dishes, I decided to make a dip similar to the traditional taghmees. Luckily, I had most of the ingredients I needed already stocked in my kitchen.

The idea was simple: blend cooked greens with yogurt to create a creamy and herbaceous dip. It's a classic recipe that's often served with warm flatbread or as a side dish with other meals. With a drizzle of olive oil, it's ready to enjoy.

Garlic-infused broccoli & labneh dip

Broccoli bil Toum w al Labneh

¼ cup | 60ml olive oil
3 large garlic cloves, peeled
   and thinly sliced
9 oz | 250g broccoli florets
1¼ cups | 350g labneh (page 23)
   or thick Greek yogurt
1 tbsp lemon juice
1 red chile, seeded and
   finely chopped
½ cup | 10g fresh dill,
   finely chopped
½ cup | 10g fresh parsley,
   finely chopped
¼ cup | 5g fresh mint leaves,
   roughly shredded
½ tsp Aleppo chile flakes
   (or regular chile flakes)
salt and black pepper
2 tsp sumac

Heat the olive oil in a small frying pan over medium-low heat. Add the garlic and cook for 3–4 minutes, being careful not to burn it—you want it to be just golden brown. Carefully transfer the garlic from the oil to a plate lined with paper towels and set both the garlic and oil aside to cool down.

Blanch the broccoli florets in boiling salted water for 2 minutes, then remove using a slotted spoon and refresh under cold water until cool. The broccoli should be bright green with a good bite.

Drain the broccoli well, roughly chop and place in a large bowl. Add the labneh or yogurt, lemon juice, chopped red chile, most of the herbs (reserving some to garnish), the chile flakes, ½ teaspoon of salt and a good grind of black pepper.

When ready to serve, spoon the broccoli mixture on to a plate, drizzle over the garlic oil and top with the reserved herbs and fried garlic. Finally, sprinkle with the sumac and serve.

Traces have been found of domesticated beets in the ancient Middle East, particularly their greens. They were also grown by ancient Egyptians, Greeks and Romans, and it is thought that they were cultivated for their roots from the Middle Ages. Beets were used to treat various conditions, especially illnesses related to the digestion and blood. It was recommended to have beets with garlic to nullify the effect of garlic breath.

At home we did not have beets as a vegetable, and I don't think many Palestinians consider this earthy sweet root vegetable to be an ingredient that can be used in cooking. The only way I had it as a kid was when other kids in the neighbourhood would set up a made-up stand of whatever they could find around their house or garden and boil the beets whole, then sell them by the piece to kids passing by, as a warm snack. Beets are one of my favorite vegetables—as a vegetable goes, it can happily be matched with other flavors, from sweet to salty, to creamy and tart. Here I have combined all these flavors into a knockout salad suitable for any meal.

Most of the components of this recipe can be made a couple of days ahead of time, then put together before serving. You can use thick yogurt instead of labneh, as well as other salty cheeses, such as goat or feta. Double or triple the amount of toasted nuts and use them to sprinkle on top of salads, soups, rice dishes and morning porridge.

Beets with cumin labneh, toasted nuts & seeds & chives

Salatet Shamander bil Labneh

2 lbs 2 oz | 1kg beets
⅔ cup | 200g labneh (page 23)
   or thick Greek yogurt
1 heaping tsp lemon zest
1 tsp ground cumin
salt and black pepper
2 tbsp apple cider vinegar
6 tbsp | 90ml olive oil
2 tbsp toasted nuts and seeds
   (page 35)
2 tbsp finely chopped fresh
   chives

For the quick pickled beets
1 golden beet (8 oz | 230g)
1 cup | 250ml water
2 tbsp apple cider vinegar
1 tsp granulated sugar
heaping ¼ tsp ground turmeric

Preheat the oven to 400°F.

Wash the beets to remove any dirt, leaving the root intact. Wrap loosely in foil and place in a roasting pan. Pour in enough water to come ¾ inch | 2cm up the beets and cook for about 60–80 minutes, until the beets are tender enough that a knife slips in easily.

While the beets are roasting, start making the pickled golden beets. Peel and very thinly slice the golden beet, using a sharp knife or mandoline. In a small saucepan, bring the water, vinegar, sugar, turmeric and ½ teaspoon of salt to a boil. Add the beet slices, then take off the heat and set aside to cool. Once it's cooled down, it's ready to use—alternatively, it can be stored in a jar or an airtight container in the fridge for up to a week.

When the roasted beets are cool enough to handle, peel them by slipping off the skins (they should come away easily). Cut each beet in half, then each half into 2 or 3 wedges, depending on the size. Set aside for 15 minutes.

Place the labneh or yogurt in a small bowl with the lemon zest, ground cumin and heaping ¼ teaspoon of salt. Mix well to combine, then set aside.

In a large bowl, whisk together the vinegar, olive oil, ½ teaspoon of salt and a good grind of black pepper. Add the cooled beet wedges and mix well to coat.

Drain some of the pickled beets on paper towels, and arrange them in and around the cooked beets. Dot with the labneh and sprinkle with the toasted nuts. Finally, scatter over the chives.

This is another of those dishes that I often make, trying to use up the ingredients I have available. I'm sure many of you have been there. You have almost a full bag of fava beans in the freezer and wonder what to do with it. I love fava beans and often think I don't cook enough with them. With this lovely dish, there isn't much cooking required.

Serve it on its own, as a side dish or as part of a mezze spread.

Serve 4–6 as a side or part of a spread

Crushed fava beans with goat cheese & preserved lemon salsa

M'tabbal Ful Akhdar

12¼ oz | 350g frozen fava beans, thawed
1 cup | 150g frozen peas, thawed
2 garlic cloves, crushed to a paste
2 tbsp lemon juice
3 tbsp olive oil
½ cup | 10g fresh mint leaves, thinly shredded, plus a few to garnish
1 green chile, seeded and finely chopped
½ cup | 10g fresh dill, finely chopped
½ cup | 10g fresh parsley, finely chopped
salt and black pepper
4¼ oz | 120g soft goat cheese, crumbled

For the salsa
1 green chile, seeded and finely chopped
1 preserved lemon, flesh removed and finely chopped (about ½ oz | 15g)
2 tbsp sumac
2 tbsp olive oil

Bring a medium saucepan of salted water to a boil, add the fava beans and peas and cook for 1 minute. Drain, rinse under cold water and set aside to drain again.

Put the beans and peas into the bowl of a food processor and pulse for about 10–15 seconds, scraping down the sides of the bowl midway. You want a fairly rough texture here. Put the garlic, lemon juice and olive oil into a medium bowl, then add the mint, chile, dill, parsley, ½ teaspoon of salt and a good grind of black pepper. Add the crushed beans and mix well.

To make the salsa, in a small bowl mix together the green chile, preserved lemon, sumac and olive oil.

Spoon the fava bean mixture on to a serving plate and spread it out a little. Top with the salsa and the crumbled goat cheese. Finish with mint leaves and a good drizzle of olive oil.

Salads

This is a great midweek supper dish and an easy way to prepare an eggplant salad. It's as simple as mixing the salsa and spooning it over the eggplant before serving.

   Apart from the time it takes to roast the eggplants, this salad takes a few minutes to make. You can also roast the eggplants the night before and finish the dish before supper.

Roasted eggplant with tomato, pomegranate & herbs

Salatet Bitinjan

1 lb 5oz | 600g baby or Japanese eggplants
6 tbsp | 90ml olive oil, plus more for drizzling
salt and black pepper
10½ oz | 300g mixed-color cherry tomatoes, halved
2 garlic cloves, crushed to a paste
½ cup | 10g fresh parsley, chopped
¼ cup | 5g fresh mint leaves, finely shredded
2 tbsp lemon juice
2 tbsp pomegranate molasses
10 basil leaves

Preheat the oven to 450°F.

Cut the eggplants lengthwise into 4 or 6 wedges, depending on their size. Arrange the wedges on a parchment-lined baking sheet and drizzle with half the olive oil. Sprinkle with ½ teaspoon of salt and a good grind of black pepper, and mix well to coat. Roast for 25 minutes, or until golden brown, then remove from the oven and allow to cool slightly while you make the salsa.

Put the tomatoes, garlic, parsley, mint and lemon juice into a medium bowl, and add the rest of the olive oil, ½ teaspoon of salt and a good grind of black pepper. Mix well and set aside.

When ready to serve, arrange the eggplant wedges on a serving plate and spoon the tomato salsa all over. Drizzle over the pomegranate molasses, a bit more olive oil and top with the basil leaves.

Sweet watermelon and salty white cheese form a timeless culinary combination deeply rooted in the food traditions of North Africa and the Middle East. It encapsulates the essence of summer, offering a symphony of flavors that tantalize the palate. It transcends borders, transporting us to idyllic seaside destinations where the sun-kissed flavors of summer reign supreme. With each bite, the refreshing sweetness of the watermelon harmonizes with the savory tang of the cheese, creating a contrast that evokes the season's warmth.

The story begins with the domestication of watermelons in north-eastern Africa, with cultivation dating back to ancient Egypt, around 2000 BCE. During Roman times, a proliferation of sweet dessert watermelons spread across the Mediterranean world, laying the foundation for this beloved pairing of watermelon and cheese.

This historical journey of flavors seamlessly connects with the traditions of Palestinian cuisine, where every ingredient tells a tale of its own. In Palestine, jibneh baladieh, which is similar to feta cheese, emerged as a prized component, embodying centuries of agricultural heritage and culinary craftsmanship. Made from fresh sheep's milk during the spring season, this cheese undergoes a meticulous curdling, draining and brining process, resulting in a distinctive flavor and texture that reflects the essence of the region.

Watermelon, cucumber salad with feta & lemon verbena

Salatet Batikh w Khyar ma' Jibneh

1 lb 2 oz | 500g watermelon, cut into small slices (about ½ a small melon)
1 cucumber, peeled and cut into chunks (about 6 oz | 180g)
1 small red onion, peeled and very thinly sliced (⅔ cup | 80g)
1 green chile, thinly sliced
1¾ oz | 50g pitted Kalamata olives
1 tbsp runny honey
1 tbsp pomegranate molasses
1 tbsp lemon juice
2 tbsp extra-virgin olive oil
salt
2½ oz | 75g feta cheese or goat cheese, crumbled
10 fresh mint leaves
10 fresh lemon verbena or basil leaves
1 tsp nigella seeds

Put the watermelon, cucumber, onion and chile into a large bowl and set aside. In a small bowl combine the olives, honey, pomegranate molasses, lemon juice, olive oil and a heaping ¼ teaspoon of salt, and stir well.

Gently toss the salad ingredients and then arrange them on a serving plate. Spoon the olive mixture on top, and sprinkle over the feta or goat cheese. Finally, scatter over the mint, lemon verbena or basil and the nigella seeds.

This version of Fattoush is close to the classic salad we all know and love, but it differs slightly from the one my mother used to make. Na'ama's Fattoush, published in *Jerusalem* and *Falastin*, is still made by my family today, and it brings me much comfort knowing her legacy lives on.

In this version, the salad uses toasted bread and is dressed with lemon and pomegranate molasses, whereas my mother's version includes a homemade buttermilk dressing and uses untoasted bread. Both are equally vibrant, crunchy, tangy and packed with fresh herbs.

Who could resist such a salad, especially when summer-ripe tomatoes, cool cucumbers and chunks of bread are brought together on one big plate.

Play around with the ingredients based on what's available in season or in your fridge. Thinly sliced red or white cabbage, kale, raw zucchini and asparagus all make great additions to this versatile dish.

Fridge-raid fattoush

Fattoush

2–3 stale whole-wheat
  pita breads
12 oz | 350g mixed-color
  tomatoes
1 large cucumber (10½ oz | 300g)
1 red pepper (5¼ oz | 150g)
1 large garlic clove, crushed to
  a paste
3 tbsp lemon juice
1½ tbsp white wine vinegar
1½ tbsp pomegranate molasses
¼ cup | 60ml olive oil
½ tsp cumin seeds, toasted and
  coarsely crushed
¾ tsp coriander seeds, toasted
  and coarsely crushed
1 tbsp sumac, plus more for
  sprinkling
salt
4¼ oz | 120g radishes, thinly sliced
1 large banana shallot, thinly
  sliced (2½ oz | 70g)
3–4 green onions, thinly sliced
1 cup | 20g fresh parsley,
  roughly chopped
¾ cup | 15g fresh mint, finely
  shredded
½ cup | 10g fresh cilantro,
  roughly chopped

Preheat the oven to 400°F.

Split open the pita and arrange them on a baking sheet, making sure they are not overlapping. Toast for 10–12 minutes, or until they are golden. Set aside to cool, then break into bite-size pieces.

Cut the large tomatoes into ½-inch | 1cm wedges and the small ones in half, and put them into a large bowl. Seed the cucumber and cut into ½-inch | 1cm cubes, then do the same with the red pepper.

Add the rest of the ingredients, apart from the bread, along with ¾ teaspoon of salt, and give everything a good mix, making sure all the vegetables are coated with the dressing.

Before serving the fattoush, add the toasted bread and give the salad another good mix. Sprinkle with sumac and serve at once.

Khyar bil laban, or cucumber in yogurt, is another staple Middle Eastern dish often served alongside rice-based dishes to cut through the richness of these and to provide a refreshing and cooling effect.

There is nothing better than a plate of two-lentil mejadra (page 169) or ouzi phyllo parcels (page 224) with a generous spoonful of this salad. I tend to use the small Middle Eastern cucumbers, when possible, because they have so much more flavor and are less watery.

Cucumber & feta yogurt with dill, almonds & rose

Khyar bil Laban

4 small Persian cucumbers
or 1 large
2 cups | 500g labneh (page 23)
or thick Greek yogurt
4¼ oz | 120g feta, crumbled
1 fat garlic clove, crushed to
a paste
2 tbsp lemon juice
1 tbsp olive oil, plus more for
drizzling
salt
1 tbsp each of fresh cilantro, dill
and mint, roughly chopped,
plus more mint to garnish
½ tsp dried mint
1 large green chile, seeded and
finely chopped
1 lime, peeled, segmented and
roughly chopped
¼ cup | 20g almonds, toasted
and roughly chopped
2 tbsp dill fronds
½ tsp nigella seeds
1 tsp dried rose petals

Peel the cucumber and cut into ¾-inch | 2cm dice (if you are using a large cucumber, cut it in half lengthwise and scoop out the middle).

Place the cucumber in a large bowl, then add the labneh or yogurt, feta, garlic, lemon juice and olive oil, ½ teaspoon of salt, the herbs, chile and lime, and mix well.

Spread the mixture on a serving plate and garnish with the almonds, dill, mint, nigella seeds and rose petals. Finish with a good drizzle of olive oil, and serve.

In recent years, wild asparagus or haluin alajram has gained popularity among Palestinians—especially in Gaza, where the tender spears are foraged in early summer for personal use or to be sold in the local markets. Most of the local asparagus grows under cactus trees. Usually, it is chopped and fried with olive oil and eggs.

Serve as a starter, as part of a spread, or as a side dish with the celeriac & tomato bake (page 185) or as part of a barbecue.

Roasted asparagus with feta, almonds & mint

Halyoun

For the dressing
¼ cup | 25g sliced almonds
2 tsp nigella seeds, slightly crushed
2 tsp lemon zest
1½ tbsp lemon juice
2 tbsp olive oil
1 small garlic clove, crushed to a paste
heaping ¼ tsp granulated sugar
salt and black pepper

For the asparagus
20 thick asparagus spears (10½ oz | 300g)
1 tbsp olive oil
2¼ oz | 60g feta cheese, crumbled
10 small fresh mint leaves
½ tsp Aleppo chile flakes (or regular chile flakes)

Preheat the oven to 375°F.

Put the almonds on a small baking pan lined with parchment paper and roast for 7 minutes or until golden brown. Transfer to a bowl and set aside while you make the dressing.

Place the rest of the dressing ingredients in a medium bowl with a heaping ¼ teaspoon of salt and ⅛ teaspoon of black pepper, and whisk well to combine.

Turn the oven temperature up to 425°F.

Break off the tough ends of the asparagus and, if they're thick, cut them in half lengthwise. Place the asparagus on a large flat baking sheet, drizzle with the olive oil, then toss to coat the asparagus completely. Spread the asparagus in a single layer and sprinkle with a heaping ¼ teaspoon of salt and a good grind of black pepper. Roast for 20–22 minutes, until tender but still crisp.

Arrange the hot spears on a large serving plate and scatter the feta on top. Add the almonds to the dressing and mix well, then spoon it all over the asparagus. Garnish with the mint leaves and a sprinkle of chile flakes.

Orange and fennel dance together in a divine harmony of flavors, intertwining sweetness with a subtle bitterness and tantalizing the taste buds. I'm a happy man snacking on orange and fennel chunks sprinkled generously with sea salt and chile flakes. I adore it when blood oranges are in season, and I try to use them as much as I can—for their flavor and beautiful color.

Serve this salad at the start of a meal, placing it in the middle of the table for everyone to tuck in or as a refreshing side that goes well with many other dishes.

Bitter leaves, fennel & orange salad

Salatet Shumar w Burtuqal

4 blood oranges or regular oranges
¼ cup | 60ml lemon juice
2 tbsp orange juice
5 tbsp | 75ml olive oil
1 tbsp pomegranate molasses
2 tsp orange blossom water
salt and black pepper
3½ oz | 100g radicchio leaves
3½ oz | 100g white or red endive (1 small endive)
½ small red onion
1 small fennel bulb
6 cups | 120g arugula
¼ cup | 5g fresh mint leaves, roughly torn
¼ cup | 5g fresh tarragon leaves
2½ oz | 70g hard goat cheese, broken into chunks
3 tbsp pomegranate seeds
3 tbsp | 25g sunflower seeds, toasted

Take each of the oranges in turn and, using a sharp knife, slice off the top and base. Now cut down the side of each orange, following its natural curve, to remove the skin and white pith. Slice the oranges into ¼-inch | ½cm slices and set aside.

To make the dressing, put the lemon juice, orange juice, olive oil, pomegranate molasses and orange blossom water into a small bowl, and add ½ teaspoon of salt and a good grind of black pepper. Whisk well and set aside.

Pull apart the radicchio and endive leaves and tear them roughly into large pieces, then place them in a large bowl. Very thinly slice the onion and fennel and add them to the leaves, along with the arugula. Pour a quarter of the dressing on the salad, along with ⅛ teaspoon of salt and a grind of black pepper, and toss well.

On a large platter, start to build the salad up, layering the leaves, oranges, goat cheese and herbs, so that all the different flavors are evenly distributed throughout the salad.

Finish with a few orange slices, some chunks of cheese and spoon the remaining dressing on top. Finally, scatter over the pomegranate and sunflower seeds.

Sheet pan recipes are a wonderful way to simplify meal preparation while maximizing flavor. By cooking everything together, the ingredients meld beautifully, creating dishes that are great to serve directly from the baking sheet. The turmeric not only imparts a rich golden tone to the cauliflower but also adds a depth of flavor. Combined with the chickpeas, it makes a satisfying and nutritious meal. The lemon yogurt adds a refreshing, creamy contrast that elevates the entire dish. Whether you're preparing a weeknight dinner or a weekend feast, this sheet pan dish is sure to impress and is a satisfying meal, bursting with color.

For vegans, replace the labneh with tahini sauce (page 32). This dish goes well with couscous fritters (page 223).

Serves 4 as a side

Turmeric cauliflower & chickpeas with lemon yogurt

Zahra ma' Hummus

1 small cauliflower, cut into
  1¼-inch | 3cm florets (keeping
  some of the tender leaves)
  (1¾ lbs | 800g)
1 x 14-oz | 400g can of chickpeas,
  drained and rinsed
4 garlic cloves, peeled but
  left whole
3 tbsp olive oil
1½ tsp ground turmeric
¾ tsp smoked paprika
½ tsp Aleppo chile flakes
  (or regular chile flakes)
salt
⅔ cup | 200g thick yogurt or
  labneh (page 23)
1 tsp lemon zest
1 tbsp lemon juice
¼ cup | 5g fresh mint leaves,
  roughly chopped
¼ cup | 5g fresh cilantro leaves,
  roughly chopped
lemon wedges, to serve

Preheat the oven to 400°F. Line a large baking sheet with parchment paper.

Put the cauliflower florets and leaves into a large bowl with the chickpeas. Add the garlic, 2 tablespoons of the olive oil, the spices and ½ teaspoon of salt. Mix well, then transfer to the prepared baking sheet. Roast for 30 minutes, turning the vegetables once halfway through the roasting, until the florets are golden brown. Remove from the oven and set aside to cool for 20 minutes.

To make the yogurt sauce, put the yogurt or labneh into a bowl, add the lemon zest and juice and a heaping ¼ teaspoon of salt, and whisk well. Spread the yogurt over the base of a large flat plate and pile the cauliflower and chickpeas on top. Drizzle with the remaining tablespoon of olive oil and scatter over the herbs. Serve with lemon wedges.

Some of my fondest childhood memories revolve around the simplest of meals, and one that stands out vividly is "maqali day," which was every Friday lunchtime. Maqali, which translates to "fry-ups," consisted of a plate of mixed fried vegetables—eggplants, cauliflower, potatoes and tomatoes—all tucked snugly inside khubz bread while they were still piping hot. A dollop of tahini sauce and a generous squeeze of lemon juice made it just the best lunch. You can find a variation of this beloved meal in my recipe for makali— grilled vegetable sandwiches (page 202).

While maqali sandwiches hold a special place in my heart, fried eggplant m'tabbal offers a twist on this beloved dish, presenting it as a salad. It's a quick and easy midweek lunch or supper, and it also makes a great addition to any meal, adding a burst of flavor and texture to the table.

Fried eggplant m'tabbal with tomato & cilantro salsa

M'tabbal Bitinjan Makli

3 medium eggplants
   (1 lb 14 oz | 850g)
salt and black pepper
¼ cup | 60g tahini paste
½ cup | 150g Greek yogurt
¼ cup | 60ml lemon juice
2 large garlic cloves, crushed
   to a paste
2 cups | 500ml sunflower oil
2 large plum tomatoes,
   coarsely grated (8 oz | 230g)
3 tbsp olive oil
½ cup | 10g fresh cilantro,
   roughly chopped

Top and tail the eggplants and cut them into ½-inch | 1½cm cubes. Place the eggplant in a large colander in your sink or over a bowl, and sprinkle with 2 teaspoons of salt. Give them a good mix and leave for 1 hour.

In the meantime, put the tahini, yogurt, 2 tablespoons of the lemon juice and the garlic into a large bowl. Add a heaping ¼ teaspoon of salt and whisk well to combine. Cover the bowl and set aside.

When the eggplant is ready, spread it on a large clean kitchen towel and pat it dry. Heat the sunflower oil in a deep pan, about 11 inches | 28cm wide, and fry the eggplant in three batches for about 5 minutes, until golden brown. Lift the eggplant pieces from the oil, using a slotted spoon, and transfer to a plate lined with paper towels. Repeat with the other two batches.

Add three-quarters of the fried eggplant to the tahini yogurt, along with ⅛ teaspoon of salt, and mix well, pressing with the back of the spoon to break down some of the large pieces. In a separate bowl, place the rest of the eggplant, the grated tomato, remaining lemon juice, 2 tablespoons of the olive oil, ⅛ teaspoon of salt and a good grind of black pepper. Mix well and set aside.

When ready to serve, spoon the eggplant salad onto a serving plate, and top with the tomato salsa, then scatter over the cilantro. Drizzle the remaining tablespoon of olive oil on top.

This is a refreshing little salad that uses winter vegetables. It goes well as a side with the two-lentil mejadra (page 169) and bulgur kubbeh (page 216)—or as part of a spread. Play around and try other winter vegetables, such as turnips, radishes, parsnips and even carrots. The salad does not keep well, so it's best to serve it as soon as it's made.

Serves 2–4

Fennel, kohlrabi & cilantro salad

Salatet Shumar w Kohlrabi

2 medium kohlrabi (6 oz | 180g)
1 large fennel bulb (7 oz | 200g)
salt and black pepper
¾ cup plus 2 tbsp | 250g Greek
  yogurt
1 green chile, seeded and
  finely chopped
1 garlic clove, crushed to a paste
1 tbsp orange zest
2 tbsp lemon juice
1 tbsp olive oil, plus more
  for drizzling
¾ cup | 15g fresh cilantro,
  roughly chopped
½ cup | 10g fresh mint leaves,
  thinly shredded
1 tsp dried mint

Peel the kohlrabi and cut them in half. Remove the green part of the fennel and cut the bulb in half lengthwise, leaving the root intact. Using a mandoline or a sharp knife, cut the kohlrabi and fennel into very thin slices. Put the sliced kohlrabi and fennel into a colander over a bowl and sprinkle with ½ teaspoon of salt. Toss well and set aside for 20 minutes.

Put the yogurt, chile, garlic, orange zest, lemon juice, olive oil, ½ teaspoon of salt and a good grind of black pepper into a large bowl and whisk well. Add the kohlrabi and fennel to the bowl, along with the cilantro and fresh mint, and mix well.

Transfer the salad to a serving plate. Sprinkle with the dried mint and add a good drizzle of olive oil.

On the final day of my visits to Jerusalem, I often make sure to pass by Bab al-Amoud (the Damascus Gate) to get a few ingredients to take back with me to London. One of these is always fresh za'atar, which I buy from the falahat (village women) who sell seasonal produce on the side of the road, down by the market in the old city.

Fresh za'atar, onion and sumac make a classic Palestinian salad, one which a few of the surrounding countries share. The star is the fresh, velvety za'atar leaves, with their distinctive taste. They are aromatic, with a fragrant and earthy aroma that's both herbal and slightly floral, similar to the flavors of thyme and oregano, with a subtle peppery tinge.

It's the perfect salad to have in the summer, when tomatoes and herbs are at their best.

Tomato, za'atar & sumac salad

Salatet Za'atar w Banadoura bil Sumac

3 large ripe tomatoes, cut
    into ¼-inch | ½cm wedges
    (14 oz | 400g)
14 oz | 400g cherry tomatoes,
    cut in half
½ red onion, finely chopped
    (½ cup | 70g)
¾ cup | 15g fresh parsley,
    finely chopped
1 tbsp sumac, plus more
    for sprinkling
3 tbsp olive oil
½ tsp lemon zest
2½ tbsp lemon juice
1 tbsp pomegranate molasses
salt
¾ cup | 15g fresh za'atar or
    oregano leaves, roughly
    chopped
3 tbsp pomegranate seeds

Put the tomatoes, red onion, parsley and sumac into a large bowl. In a smaller bowl, whisk the olive oil, lemon zest, lemon juice, pomegranate molasses and 1¼ teaspoons of salt.

Pour the dressing over the salad, add the za'atar or oregano leaves and give it a good stir. Pile the salad onto a serving platter, and sprinkle with the pomegranate seeds and more sumac.

In Palestine, we grow one type of cauliflower: zahara baladi (heirloom cauliflower). Grown in the cooler areas of the West Bank, this Palestinian local variety is a prized vegetable. The seed is sown in the spring, and it takes almost a whole year for it to mature, relying on the rain-fed farming system. It's a unique variety of cauliflower, yellow in color and with a rich, creamy, slightly mustardy flavor. It is in season for only a few weeks.

Versions of this dish can be found all over Palestine and other parts of the Middle East. The cauliflower is normally deep-fried and served piping hot, with a freshly chopped salad, tahini, and lots of bread to mop up all the juices. I have roasted the cauliflower here, for a slightly healthier version. It's delicious as a side dish or as part of a spread.

Serves 4 as a side or part of a spread

Roasted cauliflower with tahini & crushed tomatoes

Salatet Zahra bil Tahinia

2 large tomatoes (9 oz | 260g)
salt
1 tbsp apple cider vinegar
3 tbsp olive oil, plus more for drizzling
1 large cauliflower, cut into 1¼–1½-inch | 3–4cm florets (about 2 lbs 2 oz | 1kg)
1 green chile, thinly sliced
½ tsp ground cinnamon
heaping ¼ tsp ground allspice
½ tsp ground turmeric
salt and black pepper
rounded ½ cup | 150g tahini sauce (page 32)
2 tbsp | 3g fresh parsley, roughly chopped

Preheat the oven to 400°F. Line a baking sheet with parchment paper.

Cut the tomatoes in half, then use a box grater to coarsely grate them, flesh side down, discarding the skin. Drain the tomato pulp for 5 minutes in a fine sieve set over a bowl—you want about 4¼ oz | 120g of grated pulp. Discard the drained liquid, place the tomato pulp in a bowl and stir in a heaping ¼ teaspoon of salt, the vinegar, and 1 tablespoon of the olive oil, then set aside.

Put the cauliflower florets into a large bowl, along with the chile, the remaining 2 tablespoons of olive oil, the spices, ¾ teaspoon of salt and a good grind of black pepper. Mix well to coat, then spread the cauliflower in a single layer on the prepared baking sheet and roast for 25 minutes, until the cauliflower is golden brown and a little charred. Remove and set aside to cool slightly.

Spread the tahini sauce on a serving platter and arrange the cauliflower and chile on top. Spoon the grated tomato over the cauliflower, and garnish with the chopped parsley and a drizzle of olive oil.

soups

Soups hold a special place in my heart, as they do for many. Whether it's silky smooth, chunky or a simple broth with noodles, soup brings warmth and comfort at any time.

When I started thinking about the soups I wanted to include in this book, it was a difficult task, as I have cooked and eaten so many over the years. I confess that, to this day, when I feel emotional distress or am in any way unwell, all I need is a warm bowl of lentil soup to soothe and restore the soul. It works its magic—a perfect remedy.

The Palestinian kitchen is a treasure trove of soups, each one a testament to the region's culinary diversity. These soups are not just delicious but also nutritious and healthy, brimming with vegetables, grains and pulses.

Soup symbolizes a homemade dish, evoking images of pots simmering on the stove, family recipes passed down through generations and the warmth of home cooking.

One of the best things to enjoy in the summer, when tomatoes are bursting with flavor, is this refreshing dish inspired by Spanish gazpacho. Originating from Andalusia, gazpacho shares a rich history with Arab culture.

During the Moorish rule of Spain, Arab influences introduced key ingredients like tomatoes, peppers and olive oil to Spanish cuisine. Chilled soups, common in Arab cuisine, were appreciated in hot climates, probably inspiring the introduction of gazpacho to Spain. The soup highlights the enduring impact of Arab culture on Mediterranean gastronomy—a delicious example of cultural fusion, showcasing the historical and culinary exchange between Spain and the Arab world.

This soup can be made a few days in advance: it keeps well and doesn't lose color or flavor. Double the batch of soup and store it chilled in a jar; it's lovely to serve in tumblers on warm summer days.

Chilled tomato & avocado soup with burnt chile

Shorbet Banadoura w Avokado

1 lb 2 oz | 500g ripe plum
  tomatoes, cored, peeled
  and roughly chopped
4½ oz | 130g red bell pepper,
  seeded and roughly chopped
4½ oz | 130g celery, roughly
  chopped
3 garlic cloves, roughly chopped
2 tbsp olive oil
1½ tbsp apple cider vinegar
1 cup | 200ml tomato passata
1 tsp sweet paprika
salt
½ a medium ripe avocado
  (3 oz | 80g), peeled and pitted

To garnish
2 pita breads
1 tbsp olive oil
1 oz | 30g cucumber, chopped
½ a medium ripe avocado
  (3 oz | 80g), peeled, pitted
  and chopped
1 oz | 30g red bell pepper, chopped
¼ cup | 5g fresh mint leaves
burnt chile salsa (page 24)

Combine the tomatoes, red pepper, celery, garlic, olive oil, vinegar, passata, paprika and 1¾ teaspoons of salt in a blender, and blend until smooth. Add the avocado and blitz again. Pour into a bowl or pitcher (thin out as desired with ice water), then cover and chill for several hours.

Meanwhile, preheat the oven to 425°F and line a large baking sheet with parchment paper to make the pita chips. Open the pita out like books, brush with the olive oil and lay them on the baking sheet. Bake for about 10–12 minutes, until golden and crunchy. Break into bite-size shards.

Serve the soup topped with the pita chips, chopped vegetables, mint leaves and some burnt chile salsa.

This quick and hearty soup takes no longer than 30 minutes to make from start to finish.

Among the diverse versions of lentil soup found across the Middle East, this Palestinian variation holds a special place in my heart. It transports me back to chilly winter days in Jerusalem, where my family would huddle around the heater, having bowls of it together.

The beauty of this recipe doesn't end there—any leftovers can be transformed into fattet adas—lentil fatteh (page 206)—the next day. Simply reheat the soup and add chunks of bread for an equally comforting dish.

Red lentil, dried mint & lemon soup

Shorbet Adas bil Laymonn

¼ cup | 60ml olive oil, plus more
  for drizzling
1 medium onion, finely chopped
  (1¼ cups | 185g)
1 medium potato, peeled and
  cut into ½-inch | 1cm cubes
  (6⅓ oz | 180g)
1 large carrot, peeled and
  cut into ½-inch | 1cm cubes
  (6 oz | 170g)
2 celery stalks, cut into
  ¼-inch | ½cm cubes (3 oz | 90g)
1¼ cups | 250g split red lentils,
  rinsed and drained
5 cups | 1.2 liters hot vegetable stock
heaping ¼ tsp ground turmeric
2 tsp ground cumin
salt and black pepper
2 tsp dried mint, plus more
  for serving
1 tsp Aleppo chile flakes (or regular
  chile flakes), plus more for serving

To serve
2 lemons, peeled and cut
  into ¼-inch | ½cm dice
¼ cup | 5g fresh cilantro leaves
1 tsp cumin seeds, toasted and
  slightly crushed

Heat the olive oil in a large saucepan over medium heat. Add the onion and cook for 5 minutes, until softened. Stir in the potato, carrot and celery, and cook for 2 minutes more.

Add the lentils, stock, turmeric and cumin and bring to a boil, then partly cover the pan and cook over low heat for 20 minutes, until the lentils are mushy. Add 2 teaspoons of salt and a good grind of black pepper, then stir the soup and remove it from the heat. Ladle out 1 lb 10 oz | 750g of the soup into a tall jug and blitz with an immersion blender until smooth (you can also do this in a freestanding blender).

Return the blitzed soup to the pan, add the dried mint and chile flakes, and simmer gently on a low heat for 2 minutes.

To serve, ladle the soup into bowls and top with the chopped lemon, cilantro leaves, toasted cumin seeds, mint and chile flakes. Drizzle with a little olive oil and serve.

The Armenian Quarter in the Old City of Jerusalem is a renowned area rich in Armenian cultural and religious heritage. The Armenian Patriarchate of Jerusalem, established in the fourteenth century, is crucial in maintaining the Armenian Christian presence in the region, reflecting the deep historical ties between Armenians and the Holy Land.

Bethlehem's population is a diverse mix of religions and ethnic groups. According to Lara Nassar-Mitri, whose family is among the last Armenian households in the area, Bethlehem once had a thriving Armenian community. Over time, many Armenians dispersed to different parts of Palestine and beyond.

This delicately flavored soup is inspired by a recipe passed down from Lara's mother. It's refreshing and comforting, perfect served warm or chilled. You can use various herbs, such as dill, chives or cilantro, and substitute the maftoul with other grains like rice, quinoa, bulgur wheat or barley.

Jerusalemite-Armenian yogurt soup

Shorbet Laban Armaniya—Qudsiyy

3½ oz | 100g maftoul (pearl couscous), rinsed and drained
salt and black pepper
¼ cup | 60ml olive oil
1 onion, finely chopped (¾ cup | 130g)
1½ cups | 400g Greek yogurt
7 tbsp | 100ml heavy cream
1¼ cups | 300ml vegetable stock
1 large egg, lightly whisked
1 tbsp cornstarch
¼ cup | 5g fresh parsley, finely chopped
2 garlic cloves, thinly sliced

To serve
5 radishes, cut into thin matchsticks
2 tbsp finely shredded fresh mint

Put the maftoul into a small saucepan with ½ teaspoon of salt and about 3⅓ cups | 800ml of water. Bring to a boil over high heat, then decrease the heat to low and cook for 20 minutes.

While the maftoul is cooking, heat 2 tablespoons of the oil in a medium saucepan. Add the onion and cook over low heat for 10 minutes, making sure the onion does not get too much color.

Put the yogurt, cream, stock, egg and cornstarch into a medium bowl and whisk well until smooth. Take the onion off the heat and add the yogurt mixture, along with 1 teaspoon of salt and a good grind of black pepper. Return to the heat and bring the soup to a gentle simmer. Add the drained maftoul and the parsley, and keep it simmering for 5 minutes.

Now make the garlic adha: Put the remaining 2 tablespoons of olive oil and the garlic into a small frying pan and cook over a low heat for about 2 minutes or until the garlic is golden and fragrant. Pour the adha over the soup, cover the saucepan and allow it to infuse for 5 minutes. Taste and adjust the seasoning if needed.

When ready to serve, stir the soup and ladle it into four shallow bowls. Garnish with the radishes and mint.

Let me introduce all the tabbouleh enthusiasts out there to this refreshing soup. It captures the flavors of tabbouleh, but saves you the meticulous fine chopping required for the salad version— tabbouleh is a refreshing Levantine salad which is also eaten all over Palestine.

As the name suggests, this dish was born out of inspiration (or shall we say, leftovers!) from a tabbouleh salad I had made a day before as part of a dinner for friends.

Serves 4

Chilled tabbouleh soup

Shorbet Tabbouleh

⅔ cup | 120g fine bulgur wheat
1¼ cups | 300ml boiling water
1 lb 2 oz | 500g tomatoes,
   peeled and roughly chopped
1 garlic clove, crushed to a paste
½ cup | 10g fresh parsley,
   roughly chopped
¼ cup | 5g fresh mint leaves,
   roughly chopped
3 tbsp red pepper paste
   (page 29)
1 small onion, peeled and
   roughly chopped (½ cup | 80g)
1 tbsp lemon juice
¼ cup | 60ml olive oil, plus more
   for finishing
½ tsp Aleppo chile flakes
   (or regular chile flakes)
⅛ tsp ground allspice
⅛ tsp ground cinnamon
salt

To serve
1 oz | 30g cucumber, chopped
   into ¼-inch | ½cm dice
1 oz | 30g red bell pepper,
   chopped into ¼-inch | ½cm dice
¼ cup | 5g fresh parsley, finely
   chopped
¼ cup | 5g fresh mint, finely
   shredded

Put ¼ cup | 90g of the bulgur into a medium bowl with the boiling water. Cover the bowl with a plate and set aside for about 10 minutes, until all the liquid has been absorbed.

Put the rest of the soup ingredients into a blender with 1 teaspoon of salt and blitz for 1–2 minutes, until completely smooth.

Pour into a bowl, add the soaked bulgur and taste the dish to adjust the seasoning.

Cover and refrigerate for an hour (or until ready to serve).

Meanwhile, put 2 teaspoons of olive oil into a small frying pan. Add the remaining 4 tsp | 30g of bulgur and fry over medium-low heat for 3–4 minutes, until the bulgur is toasty and golden brown. Remove the pan from the heat, tip the bulgur on to a plate and set aside to cool down.

When ready to serve, ladle the soup into four shallow bowls and garnish with the chopped cucumber and bell pepper, the toasted bulgur, the herbs and a final drizzle of olive oil.

Whether you seek comfort on a cold day or a refreshing bite in warmer weather, this soup is both hearty and quick to make. For the best flavor, opt for fresh sweetcorn when in season, to fully experience its sweet and creamy taste.

This sweetcorn, bean and green cabbage soup is a versatile dish that brings together a combination of vibrant ingredients to create a tasty meal. The fresh sweetcorn kernels add a natural sweetness and a delightful crunch that perfectly complements the earthiness of the beans and the crisp texture of the green cabbage.

This soup is incredibly versatile and can be enjoyed year-round. In the colder months, it serves as a warm and comforting bowl that can be enjoyed by the fire. During warmer seasons, it can be served slightly chilled or at room temperature for a refreshing and light meal.

Sweetcorn, bean & green cabbage soup

Shorbet Dhurah w Malfoof

3 tbsp olive oil
1 large onion, finely chopped
  (1¼ cups | 180g)
2 tbsp tomato paste
1 tbsp red pepper paste
  (page 29)
1¾ cups | 320g sweetcorn
  kernels, from about 2 large
  cobs (frozen sweetcorn
  can also be used)
1 tsp paprika
1½ tsp ground cumin
salt and black pepper
5¼ oz | 150g green cabbage
  leaves, chopped into
  small pieces
1 quart | 1 liter vegetable stock
1 x 14-oz | 400g can of borlotti
  or any other white beans,
  drained and rinsed

To serve
2 tbsp chopped fresh parsley
lemon wedges
crusty bread

Heat the olive oil in a large saucepan over medium heat. Add the onion and cook for 5 minutes, until it is soft and has some color.

Add the tomato paste and red pepper paste, and cook for 1 minute, then stir in the sweetcorn, paprika, cumin, 1½ teaspoons of salt and a good grind of black pepper and cook for 3 minutes, until the corn starts to caramelize slightly.

Add the cabbage leaves and cook for a couple of minutes more, until the greens start to wilt. Add the stock and the beans to the soup. Bring to a boil, then decrease the heat to low, cover the pan and simmer for 15 minutes.

When ready to serve, ladle the soup into four shallow bowls. Garnish with the parsley and serve with lemon wedges and a side of crusty bread.

Often, wintery soups can be on the heavy side, but not this one. It's tart and peppery, and it feels nutritious and soothing.

Having grown up on a diet filled with greens, such as spinach, chard, khobeza (mallow) and molokhieh (jute), I adore them all and cannot have enough of them.

Adding lemon brightens the soup, while maftoul (pearl couscous) and chickpeas provide a creamy texture. It's incredibly easy to throw together and tastes even better the next day. Use fregola as an alternative to maftoul. Also, spinach and kale are great instead of Swiss chard.

Swiss chard & maftoul soup

Shorbet Saleq w Maftoul

7 oz | 200g maftoul
  (pearl couscous)
6⅓ cups | 1.5 liters water
2 tbsp olive oil
1 large onion, chopped
1 bunch of Swiss chard (about
  10 leaves), chopped, including
  ribs (7 oz | 200g)
heaping ¼ tsp baharat (page 39)
salt and black pepper
3 tbsp tomato paste
3 tbsp lemon juice
1 x 14-oz | 400g can of chickpeas,
  drained and rinsed
1 tbsp tahini paste (optional)

Rinse the maftoul a few times and set aside.

Bring the water to a boil in a large pan and leave on the stove to keep hot.

Heat the oil in a pan, then add the onion and sauté until softened. Add the Swiss chard and sauté until tender.

Add the maftoul, baharat, 2 teaspoons of salt, a heaping ¼ teaspoon of black pepper and the tomato paste and mix well. Pour in the boiling water. When the mixture returns to a boil, decrease to low heat and simmer.

About 20 minutes later, add the lemon juice and chickpeas. Continue to simmer for 5 more minutes, or until the maftoul is tender. Add more salt, pepper and lemon juice to taste if you like.

To see if you like the addition of tahini, you can serve a small bowl of the soup, add a touch of tahini and stir. If you like the tahini in the soup, add 1 tablespoon of it to the pot and stir.

Kubbet al raheb, "monk's kubbeh" in Arabic, is a traditional dish with
roots dating back to biblical times. It is commonly enjoyed during
Lent and on Good Friday by Christian Palestinians.

   This lemony soup, with soft bulgur dumplings, holds a special
place in the traditions of many families. Preparing this soulful dish
is a culinary legacy that lives on through the generations.

Bulgur wheat dumpling & lentil soup

Kubbet al Raheb

For the dumplings
½ cup | 100g fine brown
   bulgur wheat
about 2 cups | 500ml cold water
¼ cup | ¾ oz | 25g all-purpose
   flour
½ small onion, very finely
   chopped (¼ cup | 35g)
¼ cup | 5g fresh mint leaves,
   finely shredded
1 tbsp chopped fresh basil
heaping ¼ tsp ground allspice
½ tsp sweet paprika
heaping ¼ tsp Aleppo chile flakes
   (or regular chile flakes)
salt and black pepper

For the soup
½ cup | 100g green or brown
   lentils, rinsed and drained
2 tbsp olive oil
1 medium onion, finely chopped
   (1¼ cups | 180g)
3 garlic cloves, crushed to
   a paste
3½ cups | 900ml vegetable stock
5 oz | 140g Swiss chard leaves,
   finely chopped
2 tbsp lemon juice
2 tbsp chopped fresh parsley

To make the dumplings, put the bulgur into a medium bowl and cover with the cold water. Set aside to soak for 20 minutes, until the bulgur is soft.

Once the bulgur has softened, drain and squeeze well to remove any excess water. Return the bulgur to the same bowl and add the rest of the dumpling ingredients, along with ½ teaspoon of salt and a grind of black pepper.

Knead the mixture with your hands to form a moist, sticky mixture. If it is dry, add a touch of water. Keep kneading until you have a dough-like consistency. Form the mixture into 16 round balls, about ½ oz | 17g each, and arrange the balls on a flat plate. Cover and chill for 10 minutes.

To make the soup, put the lentils into a small bowl and cover with cold water. Set aside to soak for 10 minutes.

Put the olive oil into a large saucepan and place over medium heat. Once hot, add the onion and cook for 5 minutes, until soft, then add the garlic and cook for 1 minute or until fragrant.

Add the drained lentils and the stock, and bring to a boil. Cover, lower the heat and cook for 20 minutes, until the lentils have softened. Add the dumplings one at a time and gently stir them around. Add the Swiss chard leaves, along with ¾ teaspoon of salt and a good grind of black pepper. Bring everything to a boil, pop on the lid and simmer over low heat for 20 minutes, until the soup has thickened and the dumplings are soft.

When ready to serve the soup, stir in the lemon juice. Divide the soup between four deep bowls and sprinkle with parsley.

Whether you're looking for a comforting midweek meal or an impressive starter, this soup, with its vivid green color and silky texture, is the perfect choice. Both elements can be prepared in advance, and the soup keeps well in the fridge for up to 3 days, or longer in the freezer.

Consider doubling the batch of za'atar breadcrumbs and storing them in a sealed container for use later. They are great to sprinkle over pasta, salads and roasted vegetables.

Lemony spinach soup with za'atar breadcrumbs

Shorbet Sabanikh bil Laymonn

¼ cup | 60ml olive oil, plus more
  for drizzling
2 leeks, white and light green parts,
  roughly chopped (12 oz | 350g)
2 celery stalks, roughly chopped
  (3 oz | 90g)
3 garlic cloves, crushed to a paste
2 sprigs of fresh oregano
2 bay leaves
2 large potatoes, peeled and
  cut into ¾-inch | 2cm chunks
  (10½ oz | 300g)
5½ cups | 1.3 liters vegetable stock
salt and black pepper
1 lb | 450g frozen chopped
  spinach, thawed
1 cup | 20g fresh cilantro,
  roughly chopped
¾ cup | 15g fresh parsley,
  roughly chopped
2 tbsp lemon juice

For the za'atar breadcrumbs
2 tbsp olive oil
½ cup | 50g panko breadcrumbs
  (try with fried quinoa, see note)
2 tbsp za'atar
heaping ¼ tsp Aleppo chile flakes
  (or regular chile flakes)

To serve
lemon wedges

Heat the olive oil in a large saucepan over medium-high heat. Add the leeks and celery, and cook, stirring often, for 10 minutes, until the vegetables are tender. Stir in the garlic, oregano and bay leaves, and cook for 1 minute more. Add the potatoes, stock, 2½ teaspoons of salt and a good grind of black pepper. Bring to a boil, then decrease the heat to low and simmer, partly covered, for 20 minutes, until the potatoes are soft.

Meanwhile, put all the ingredients for the za'atar breadcrumbs (or quinoa) into a medium pan and cook, stirring often, over medium heat for 5 minutes, or until the breadcrumbs are golden brown. Tip the mixture on to a flat plate and set aside to cool down.

Discard the oregano and bay leaves from the soup. Add the spinach, cilantro and parsley, and cook for 3 minutes or until the spinach has wilted. Using an immersion blender, blitz the soup until very smooth. You can also do this in batches using a freestanding blender.

When ready to serve, add the lemon juice to the soup and give it a good stir. Ladle the soup into bowls and sprinkle with a spoonful of za'atar breadcrumbs and a good drizzle of olive oil. Serve with the rest of the za'atar breadcrumbs and lemon wedges.

Note: To make the breadcrumbs with quinoa, place ¼ cup | 50g of quinoa in a small saucepan and toast for 3 minutes, shaking the pan a few times. Add enough water to cover and bring to a boil. Cover the pan and cook over very low heat for 10 minutes, until the liquid has been absorbed. Transfer the cooked quinoa to a paper towel–lined plate to absorb any excess moisture. Use the same way as the panko.

Freekeh is a type of ancient grain made from green durum wheat
that is harvested while young, roasted and rubbed to create its unique
flavor and texture. It is high in fiber and protein, making it a great
addition to soups.

Freekeh's rich history and cultural significance in the Middle East
reflect its permanent value as a nutritious and versatile grain. Its
accidental discovery and long-standing use in traditional dishes
highlight the innovative ways ancient cultures adapted to challenges
and made use of available resources. Today, freekeh continues to be
a symbol of resilience and a testament to the rich culinary heritage
of Palestine and other parts of the Middle East.

The beauty of this dish lies in its simplicity. Freekeh and vegetable
soup is a delicious and wholesome dish that's perfect as a hearty meal.

Serves 6

Freekeh & vegetable soup

Shorbet Freekeh ma' al Khudar

¾ cup | 150g cracked freekeh
3 tablespoons olive oil, plus
    more for drizzling
1 large onion, finely chopped
    1 cup | 150g
2–3 large celery stalks, cut
    into ¼-inch | ½cm cubes
    (7 oz | 200g)
2 medium carrots, peeled
    and cut into ¼-inch | ½cm
    cubes (1½ cups | 200g)
3 garlic cloves, crushed to
    a paste
1½ cups | 1 liter vegetable stock
2 medium zucchini, cut into
    ½cm cubes (14 oz | 400g)
2 tsp chopped fresh za'atar or
    oregano leaves
salt and black pepper
heaping ¼ tsp Aleppo chile flakes
    (or regular chile flakes)

To garnish
chopped fresh herbs (parsley,
    chives, green onions or more
    za'atar)

Put the freekeh into a fine sieve and rinse well under running water.
Transfer to a medium bowl, cover with plenty of cold water and set
aside to soak for 15 minutes.

Heat the olive oil in a large saucepan over medium heat. Add the
onion and cook, stirring, until softened—about 7 minutes. Add the
celery and carrots and cook, stirring for 5 minutes. Add the garlic
and cook for 1 more minute.

Drain the freekeh and add it to the pan along with the stock,
zucchini, za'atar or oregano leaves, 1½ teaspoons of salt, a good
grind of black pepper and the chile flakes.

Bring the soup to a boil, then decrease the heat to low and simmer,
uncovered, for 25–30 minutes or until the vegetables are completely
soft and the soup has thickened.

When ready to serve, ladle the soup into bowls, garnish with the
herbs and drizzle with olive oil.

158   Soups

weekday dinners

Despite dedicating most of my adult life to cooking professionally, I still love cooking at home. After a long day in the kitchen, I often pick up a few ingredients on my way home, to make something for Jeremy and me or if we have friends over.

Like many chefs, I don't usually enjoy eating the food I cook at work outside of work, so on weekdays I follow my mood when deciding what to cook. I don't plan much in advance, and I often choose what I feel like eating and cooking at the last minute. Other times, I go to one of my local shops and inspiration comes from seeing what's available in season at the time of year.

Most of our weekday meals are designed to be easy and straightforward. However, during particularly busy periods, I tend to prepare dishes a day or two in advance to heat or finish when needed.

In this chapter, you'll find great weekday dishes. Some are pretty easy to rustle up and are intended to make your midweek meal a breeze, and others take longer, so they need a bit of planning.

Each recipe is designed to be straightforward to follow, delivering a mouthwatering dish. Like the proverbial promise on the tin, these recipes live up to their claims, ensuring that what you see is what you get.

Whether you're craving a comforting celeriac & tomato bake (page 185), a soothing rice & lentils wet pilaf (page 186) or fried halloumi with purslane salad (page 164), you can trust that these recipes will deliver satisfying results every time.

This dish is designed to be quick and easy, allowing you to enjoy fresh, tasty halloumi cheese and a salad in just a few minutes. It's a lifesaver when I need a no-fuss, wholesome meal. I am consistently drawn to this squeaky and refreshing combination, whether for lunch or dinner. I guarantee you'll be tempted to recreate it time and time again.

If you don't have a grill pan, you can fry the cheese until crispy or place it under a hot broiler. The halloumi can also be cut into chunks after cooking and scattered over the salad.

Fried halloumi with purslane salad

Halloum Maklyeh ma' Salatet Baqleh

2 x 8 oz | 225g packets of
 halloumi (plain)
¼ cup | 60ml olive oil, plus more
 for drizzling
1 tbsp apple cider vinegar
1½ tbsp runny honey
salt and black pepper
10½ oz | 300g cherry plum
 tomatoes, cut in half
10½ oz | 300g cucumber,
 large seeds removed
3 oz | 80g purslane, mâche
 or mixed leaves
¼ cup | 5g fresh mint leaves
½ cup | 10g fresh basil leaves
¼ cup | 5g fresh oregano leaves
heaping ¼ tsp Aleppo chile flakes
 (or regular chile flakes)
1½ tsp za'atar
½ cup | 60g sumac onions
 (page 33)

Cut each halloumi block in half horizontally, separating the two halves, then cut each in half again so that you have 8 slices of halloumi. Pat dry, then place on a large plate and brush with about 1 tablespoon of olive oil. Heat a grill pan until very hot and grill the cheese for 3 minutes on each side. Resist the temptation to move the pieces of halloumi until they are ready to turn, and lift them carefully when you do, so that the charred marks stay intact.

In a large bowl, whisk the remaining 3 tablespoons of oil, the vinegar, honey, a heaping ¼ teaspoon of salt and a good grind of black pepper. Add the tomatoes, cucumber, leaves and herbs and give the salad a good mix.

When ready to serve, drizzle the cheese with a little olive oil and sprinkle with the chile flakes and za'atar. Divide the salad between four plates and top with the sumac onions. Arrange two pieces of halloumi on each plate and serve at once.

Artichokes are available throughout spring and often in autumn, and Palestinians make the most of their season.

I must admit, I'm a bit lazy when it comes to cooking with large artichokes because of the amount of work they require to prepare and cook. Saying that, I love the smaller purple (violet) ones, and I'm always happy to buy a bunch or two, as they're easier to prepare and have more of a flavor to them, not much choke to remove and most of the leaves are edible.

Always choose fresh-looking artichokes with firm stems and no brown spots.

For this dish, all the chopping and cleaning can be done a day before, and it can be put together in no time.

Serve with fattoush (page 117) and tahini sauce (page 32). Any leftovers can be tossed into a leafy salad and sprinkled with toasted nuts & seeds (page 35).

Artichoke & potato in olive oil & preserved lemon

Yakhni Ardi Shauki wa Batata

2 lemons
10 baby violet or 4 large globe
    artichokes (2½ lbs | 1.2kg)
6–7 medium baby potatoes, cut
    into quarters (1 lb 5 oz | 600g)
10 large garlic cloves, peeled and
    cut into quarters, lengthwise
3 sprigs of fresh oregano
5 sprigs of fresh thyme
3 sprigs of fresh parsley
1 green chile, cut into 4 pieces
6 cups | 1½ liters water
3 tbsp apple cider vinegar
salt and black pepper
½ cup plus 2 tbsp | 150ml olive oil

For the salsa
2 tbsp preserved lemon,
    finely chopped
3 tbsp | 20g capers,
    roughly chopped
¼ cup | 5g fresh parsley,
    finely chopped
1 tbsp olive oil

To prepare the artichokes, fill a large bowl with cold water, squeeze in the juice of one of the lemons and drop in the skins too (this is to prevent the cut surfaces of the artichokes from discoloring). Squeeze the other lemon to make 3 tablespoons of juice and set aside.

If the artichokes have long stems, cut most of the stem off, leaving about 2 inches | 5cm at the base. Remove a few of the outer leaves and cut the artichokes in half through the stem and heart, then use a teaspoon to scrape away the choke. Rub the cut surfaces all over with the used lemon halves and put them into the bowl of water.

Put the prepared artichokes, potatoes, garlic, herbs and chile into a large deep pan with a lid, about 12 inches | 30cm in diameter, and add the water, lemon juice, vinegar and 1 tablespoon of salt. Bring to a boil over a high heat, then cover the pan and cook over medium heat for 22 minutes, until the potatoes are cooked through.

Remove the herbs, then carefully pour away most of the cooking liquid, leaving about 1¼ cups | 300ml behind in the pan. Return the pan to the heat. Add the olive oil, 1¼ teaspoons of salt and a good grind of black pepper, and cook uncovered for 10 minutes, stirring a couple of times, until most of the water has evaporated. Remove the pan from the heat and allow it to cool down for 10 minutes.

Put all the salsa ingredients into a small bowl and mix well. Sprinkle the salsa on top of the vegetables. Serve straight from the pan or transfer to a serving platter.

Here's a slightly different and somewhat easier version of the beloved Palestinian dish mejadra, a cherished favorite from my childhood. This version brings back memories of fragrant spices mingling with the sweet aroma of fried onions, which filled the air whenever this was prepared. I fondly recall my dad packing us and a big pot of mejadra to go on a picnic, escaping the heat of Jerusalem for a cooler spot in the countryside.

   Whether eaten hot or at room temperature, the combination of flavors is as comforting as can be. The roasted onion, turned into a salsa to top the dish, is key and shouldn't be skipped. Serve with some freshly made chopped salad.

Two-lentil mejadra

Mejadara

1 cup | 200g Egyptian or
   short-grain rice
¾ cup | 150g green lentils,
   rinsed and drained
½ cup | 100g red lentils,
   rinsed and drained
2 tsp cumin seeds
1½ tbsp coriander seeds
2 tbsp olive oil
2 tsp tomato paste
½ tsp ground turmeric
1½ tsp ground allspice
1½ tsp ground cinnamon
1½ cups | 375ml cold water

For the salsa
2–3 large onions (1 lb 3 oz | 530g)
2 tbsp olive oil
salt and black pepper
⅓ cup | 7g fresh parsley,
   finely chopped
¼ cup | 5g fresh mint,
   finely shredded
4 green onions, finely
   sliced (1¾ oz | 50g)
2 tsp sumac
2 tsp lemon juice

To serve
3 tbsp | 3g fresh parsley leaves
1 tsp sumac
Greek yogurt

Preheat the oven to 375°F. Line a large baking sheet with parchment paper.

To make the salsa, peel the onions and cut them into wedges (¾ inch | 2cm at the thickest point). Place them in a large bowl and toss them with 1 tablespoon of olive oil, a heaping ¼ teaspoon of salt and a grind of black pepper until coated. Place in a single layer on the prepared baking sheet and roast for 45 minutes, until soft, golden and starting to caramelize. Take out of the oven and set aside.

Meanwhile, rinse the rice well and place in a small bowl, add enough cold water to cover and set aside to soak for 10 minutes. Put the lentils into a small lidded saucepan, cover with plenty of water, bring to a boil and cook for 10 minutes, or until the green lentils have softened but still have a little bite (the red lentils will cook quicker and collapse at this point). Drain in a colander.

Place a 10-inch | 24cm sauté pan over a medium heat and toast the cumin and coriander seeds for a minute or two, until fragrant. Add 2 tablespoons of oil, the tomato paste and the spices—stir for a minute or two to combine, then add the drained rice, the lentils, the water, 1½ teaspoons of salt and a good grind of black pepper. Stir well to combine, then bring to a boil. Cover, turn the heat down to very low, and simmer for 15 minutes.

Remove from the heat, lift off the lid and cover the pan with a clean kitchen towel. Seal tightly with the lid and set aside for 15 minutes.

Put the cooked onion wedges into a medium bowl, add the remaining 1 tablespoon of olive oil and the rest of the salsa ingredients and mix well.

When ready to serve, remove the lid and kitchen towel from the mejadra and place a large flat plate over the open pan. Carefully but quickly invert the pan, holding both sides firmly. Leave the pot on the plate for 2 minutes, then slowly lift it off. Top with the salsa, scatter over the parsley leaves and sprinkle with the sumac. Serve with yogurt.

The inspiration for this recipe comes from the traditional Palestinian stuffed carrots simmered in a rich, garlic-infused tamarind broth. However, the aim is to offer a quicker alternative by skipping the coring, stuffing and long cooking time required for the original recipe without compromising the flavor. This dish delivers bold flavors without complex preparation.

Serve warm or at room temperature. While grilling enhances the dish's smoky undertones, it remains delicious even without this step (just cook the carrots a little longer). Serve with rice or crusty bread, and tahini sauce (page 32).

Carrots in tamarind & mint

Jazar bil Tamer Hindi

2⅓ oz | 65g solid tamarind paste
7 tbsp | 100ml boiling water
2 lbs 2 oz | 1kg carrots
  (medium size), peeled and
  cut in half lengthwise
¼ cup | 60ml olive oil
6 garlic cloves, crushed to
  a paste
1 tsp dried mint
10 cardamom pods, lightly
  crushed
½ tsp ground cinnamon
½ tsp Aleppo chile flakes
  (or regular chile flakes)
1½ tsp coriander seeds, lightly
  crushed
½ tsp granulated sugar
salt and black pepper
¾ cup plus 2 tbsp | 200ml
  boiling water

To serve
¼ cup | 5g fresh mint leaves
¼ cup | 5g fresh cilantro leaves

Place the tamarind paste in a bowl and pour over the boiling water. Set aside for 20 minutes or so, stirring or squeezing the pulp into the water from time to time. Pass the tamarind mixture through a fine-mesh sieve into a bowl. Discard the seeds and pulp left over in the sieve.

In a large bowl, toss the carrots with 1 tablespoon of the olive oil until well coated. Heat a grill pan over high heat and cook the carrots for 3 minutes on each side, without moving them, until they get nicely charred marks.

Put the remaining 3 tablespoons of oil into a large deep-sided sauté pan, one which has a lid. Add the garlic and fry for a minute over medium heat, stirring frequently, then add the dried mint and spices and cook for another 30 seconds. Add the carrots, the tamarind liquid, sugar, 1½ teaspoons of salt, a grind of black pepper and the water. Stir well to combine, cover with a lid, then decrease the heat to low and cook for 35 minutes, until the sauce has thickened and the carrots are cooked through.

Transfer the carrots to a serving plate and scatter the mint and cilantro on top just before serving.

During the spring, when fava beans are at their peak tenderness and flavor, there's no need to go through the tedious task of shelling and peeling them. Choose the smallest, thinnest beans, simply trim the ends, and slice them as they are. Frozen fava beans are fine to use.

The beauty of this dish is that it is super easy to make and packed full of flavor. Ful akhdar makes a great main, and it can also be a side or part of a spread.

Serves 4 as a main or 6 as a side

Fava beans with lemon & cilantro

Ful Akhdar

2 large lemons
⅓ cup | 80ml olive oil
1 onion, finely chopped
  (1 cup | 150g)
salt and black pepper
1 lb 5 oz | 600g fresh fava
  beans, trimmed and cut into
  1¼-inch | 3cm pieces
6 garlic cloves, crushed to
  a paste
2 cups | 500ml vegetable stock
1½ cups | 30g fresh cilantro,
  roughly chopped

Zest one of the lemons (to get about 1 tablespoon of zest), then peel both lemons, making sure to remove any white pith). Cut the flesh into ¼-inch | ½cm chunks, discarding any seeds as you go; put both zest and flesh into a small bowl and set aside.

Heat 3 tablespoons of the olive oil in a large pan (one for which you have a lid), then add the onion and ½ teaspoon of salt and cook over medium heat, stirring occasionally, for 5 minutes, until the onion is soft. Mix in the beans and cook for a further 5 minutes, then add the garlic, stock, 1¼ teaspoons of salt and a good grind of black pepper. Bring everything to a boil, then cover and cook over low heat for 20 minutes. Remove the pan from the heat and add the cilantro, chopped lemon and lemon zest, and the remaining olive oil.

Serve warm or at room temperature, with rice, bulgur wheat or bread.

The Palestinian equivalent of egg and chips is batata w beyd, or muba'atra, yet another simple dish that's commonly enjoyed as a hearty and comforting meal. It's a simple yet fulfilling dish, made with basic ingredients that are easily accessible at home.

Batata w beyd is often served as a main dish, accompanied by a side of chopped vegetables, pickles, shatta and bread. Perfect for breakfast, lunch or dinner, its simplicity makes it a popular choice for home cooks looking to prepare a quick and satisfying meal.

Palestinian egg & chips

Batata w Beyd

4 large potatoes (2½ lbs | 1.2kg)
¼ cup | 60ml plus 1 tsp sunflower oil
2 tbsp | 30g butter
salt and black pepper
2 medium onions, finely chopped (2 cups | 300g)
8 medium eggs
1½ tsp sumac
2 tbsp fresh parsley, roughly chopped
2 tbsp fresh oregano leaves
olive oil

Peel the potatoes and cut them into ½-inch | 1½cm cubes.

Heat ¼ cup | 60ml of the sunflower oil and the butter in a very large frying pan and add the potato cubes, 1 teaspoon of salt and ¾ teaspoon of black pepper. Cook over medium-high heat, stirring a few times, for 17 minutes, or until the potatoes are crisp, golden brown and soft within. Remove the potatoes from the pan and set aside.

Using the same pan, decrease the heat to medium, then add the teaspoon of sunflower oil and the onion. Cook, stirring, until the onion is soft and light golden, about 5 minutes. Return the potatoes to the pan and stir a couple of times.

Crack in the eggs and cook until they are cooked through, with the yolks still slightly runny, 8–10 minutes. You can cover the pan with a lid for the last few minutes (to speed up the process).

Sprinkle the dish with a bit more salt, the sumac and the herbs, and finish with a final drizzle of olive oil.

There are many kinds of eggplant and tomato dishes in the Middle East, each with its own distinct character, and this eggplant and chickpea stew is no exception. It's a hearty dish that combines the meatiness of the eggplant, the nutty-creamy texture of the chickpeas and the umami of the tomato sauce, all complemented by the zesty green chile sauce.

You can serve this as it is, with simple rice, or as a base for a pasta bake or shakshuka. The dish tastes even better the next day, making it convenient to prepare in advance. Just keep the green chile sauce separate and reheat the stew before serving.

Eggplant & chickpeas with green lemon sauce

Bitinjan ma' Hummus

2 medium eggplants, cut
 into 1¼-inch | 3cm chunks
 (1 lb 5 oz | 600g)
6 tbsp | 90ml olive oil
salt and black pepper
1 large onion, finely chopped
 (1⅔ cups | 240g)
2 celery stalks, cut into
 ½-inch | 1cm dice (5½ oz | 160g)
1 red pepper, cut into
 ½-inch | 1cm dice (6 oz | 180g)
8 garlic cloves, crushed to
 a paste
2 tsp ground cumin
1 tsp ground coriander
½ tsp ground cinnamon
1 tsp Aleppo chile flakes
 (or regular chile flakes)
1 tsp paprika
½ tsp ground allspice
½ tsp ground turmeric
2 x 14-oz | 400g cans of diced
 tomatoes
2 x 14-oz | 400g cans of
 chickpeas, drained and rinsed
1¼ cups | 300ml water

To serve
1 recipe green lemon sauce
 (page 28; replace half
 the parsley with cilantro)

Preheat the oven to 450°F.

Toss the eggplant chunks in 2 tablespoons of the oil, and season with a heaping ¼ teaspoon of salt and a good grind of black pepper. Roast for 22–24 minutes, until soft and golden brown.

While the eggplant is roasting, make the sauce. Heat the remaining olive oil in a large, lidded sauté pan. Add the onion and fry over medium heat for about 5 minutes, until softened.

Add the celery and red pepper and continue to cook for another 6 minutes. Add the garlic and spices and cook for another minute or so, until fragrant.

Add the tomatoes, chickpeas, cooked eggplant and the water and season with 1½ teaspoons of salt and a grind of black pepper. Bring everything to a boil, then turn down the heat, cover and cook for about 20 minutes, until the eggplant chunks have softened and the flavors have come together.

Allow to cool slightly, then serve in bowls with the green lemon sauce.

Baked sweet potatoes make a great midweek meal or a weekend brunch. They're delicious topped with creamy beans, tangy cheese and nutty tahini, with a sharp green chile sauce to balance the richness.

I love how all the flavors work together here. There's room to play with other ingredients you have to hand, such as hummus, toasted nuts and seeds, leftover grains and veggies.

This dish can be a meal alone, served with a fresh green salad or as a side. Serve it in the roasting dish and place it in the middle of the table for everyone to help themselves.

Loaded sweet potatoes with black-eyed peas

Batata Helweh ma' Loubia

2½ lbs | 1.2kg sweet potatoes
  (about 4 medium)
2 garlic cloves, crushed to
  a paste
2 tbsp olive oil
heaping ¼ tsp ground cumin
⅛ tsp ground cinnamon
1 x 14-oz | 400g tin of black-eyed
  peas, drained and rinsed
7 tbsp | 100ml water
salt and black pepper

For the toppings
3½ oz | 100g cherry tomatoes,
  roughly chopped
1½ tbsp olive oil
2 tbsp | 2½g fresh parsley,
  finely chopped, plus more
  leaves to garnish
2 tbsp | 2½g fresh mint leaves,
  finely sliced, plus more leaves
  to garnish
1 tbsp lemon juice
flaked sea salt
tahini sauce (page 32)
green lemon sauce (page 28)
olive oil

Preheat the oven to 425°F.

Scrub the sweet potatoes, pat them dry and cut them in half lengthwise. Place them on a parchment-lined baking sheet flesh side down, cover with foil and cook for 30 minutes, then unwrap and let them cook uncovered for 30–40 minutes more (depending on the size of the potatoes), until soft.

Meanwhile, heat the garlic and oil gently in a medium saucepan over medium-low heat for 2 minutes, until the garlic is soft but not browned. Add the spices and cook for a further minute, then add the peas, water, a heaping ¼ teaspoon of salt and a grind of black pepper. Cook, stirring gently, for about 20 minutes, until the liquid has reduced. Roughly mash some of the peas, so that the sauce thickens. Set aside.

Put the tomatoes into a small bowl, then add the oil, chopped herbs, lemon juice and a pinch of salt. Stir and set aside.

When the potatoes are done, take them out of the oven, turn them flesh side up and sprinkle with a little flaked sea salt.

Top with a couple spoonfuls of peas, a spoonful of tahini sauce, the tomatoes, some green lemon sauce and finally some mint and parsley leaves, roughly torn. Finish with a little more flaked sea salt and a drizzle of olive oil. Serve immediately.

I deeply admire this knobbly, humble root vegetable—especially its delicate, earthy flavor. Celeriac can transform dishes with its distinctive flavor, which is similar to celery but with a milder, nuttier undertone. It works really well here with the rest of the ingredients, composing the perfect vegetable bake to enjoy with a leafy salad.

Roast the celeriac and make the sauce a day before, but keep them apart, then finish in the dish before serving.

Celeriac & tomato bake

Karfs w Banadoura bil Furn

2 medium celeriac, peeled and cut into 2 x 1¼-inch | 5 x 3½cm chunks (2 lbs 2 oz | 1kg)
5 tbsp | 75ml olive oil
salt and black pepper
2 large red onions, thinly sliced (heaping 2 cups | 260g)
4 garlic cloves, crushed to a paste
1¼ tsp ground cinnamon
½ tsp ground allspice
½ tsp Aleppo chile flakes (or regular chile flakes)
1 tsp coriander seeds
1 tsp cumin seeds
1½ tbsp sumac
1 x 14-oz | 400g can of diced tomatoes
2 eggs
2–3 green onions, thinly sliced (1 oz | 30g)
4¼ oz | 120g hard goat cheese, coarsely grated

Preheat the oven to 425°F. Line a baking sheet with parchment paper.

Place the celeriac in a large bowl and add 3 tablespoons of the olive oil, ½ teaspoon of salt and a good grind of black pepper. Mix well, then transfer to the prepared baking sheet. Roast for about 40 minutes, or until the celeriac is golden brown and cooked through.

While the celeriac is cooking, put the rest of the olive oil into a large ovenproof sauté pan. Add the onions and fry over medium-high heat for 7 minutes, until slightly colored and soft. Add the garlic and spices and cook for 1 minute more, until fragrant. Add the tomatoes, ½ teaspoon of salt and a good grind of black pepper, then decrease the heat to medium and cook for another 5 minutes.

Add the cooked celeriac to the tomato sauce and mix to combine. Whisk the eggs in a medium bowl, add the green onions and half the goat cheese, and give everything a good mix. Pour the egg mixture over the vegetables and sprinkle the rest of the cheese on top. Roast for 25 minutes, until the top is golden.

Serve at once.

Sha'aktoura is a versatile traditional Palestinian dish originating from Hebron, in the southern West Bank. This dish can be prepared in various ways. It is often served as a pilaf or, alternatively, as a soup.

The key ingredient in sha'aktoura is khobiza, also known as common mallow, a wild green that flourishes in the spring. When khobiza is not in season, spinach is an excellent substitute, having a similar texture and flavor.

This recipe is somewhere between a pilaf and a soup, similar in consistency to a risotto, which is why it is called a wet pilaf. It combines the heartiness of a pilaf with the comfort of a risotto.

Sha'aktoura is a quick and flavorful way to feed the family, providing a filling meal that's bursting with taste.

Rice & lentils wet pilaf

Sha'aktoura

1 quart | 1 liter water
salt and black pepper
¾ cup plus 2 tbsp | 175g Egyptian
  or other short-grain rice
¾ cup | 160g split red lentils
3 tbsp olive oil
1 onion, finely chopped
  (¾ cup | 20g)
5 garlic cloves, crushed to a paste
1 green chile, finely chopped
1 oz | 30g fresh ginger, finely grated
1½ tsp cumin seeds, toasted and
  finely crushed
1½ tsp coriander seeds, toasted
  and finely crushed
¾ tsp ground cinnamon
½ tsp ground turmeric
2 tbsp tomato paste
1¼ cups | 300ml water
1 lb 2 oz | 500g frozen spinach,
  thawed
1¼ cups | 25g fresh cilantro,
  roughly chopped
1 cup | 20g fresh mint, roughly
  chopped, plus some whole
  leaves to serve
3 tbsp lemon juice

Pour the water into a medium, lidded saucepan, then add ½ teaspoon of salt and bring to a boil. Rinse the rice and lentils and add them to the boiling water, bring back to a boil, then lower the heat and simmer for 20 minutes, until the rice is cooked and the lentils are completely mushy. Take off the heat and set aside.

Put the olive oil into a large sauté pan and place over medium-high heat. Add the onion and cook for about 10 minutes, stirring a few times, until soft and nicely browned. Add the garlic, chile and ginger and cook for another minute, until fragrant.

Add the spices and tomato paste and cook for 2 minutes more, then add the cooked rice and lentils, the water, 1 teaspoon of salt and a good grind of black pepper. Bring to a boil, then add the spinach, chopped herbs and lemon juice. Cook for 2–3 minutes and serve immediately topped with some mint leaves.

This keeps well in the fridge for up to 3 days, making it convenient for packed lunches and easy weeknight dinners.

The inspiration for this dish came from the fried cauliflower with tahini which is a loved dish in Palestinian cuisine. Bil siniyhe translates to "in a tray" or "roasted in a tray" in Arabic.

Here, cabbage and onion are slow-cooked until meltingly caramelized, tender and sweet. This is a delicious way of cooking cabbage—first you sear it in the pan, then add layers of flavors that complement its sweet caramelized taste as well as the creaminess and nuttiness of the tahini. You can replace the tahini with a mixture of Parmesan and mozzarella to turn the dish into a gratin.

Pointy cabbage & tahini bil siniyhe

Malfoof bil Siniyeh

¼ cup | 60ml olive oil, plus more
  for drizzling
2 pointy (or hispi/conehead)
  cabbages, or 1 large white
  cabbage, cut into quarters,
  leaving the core intact
  (1¾ lb | 800g)
salt and black pepper
2 red onions, peeled and thinly
  sliced (scant 2 cups | 220g)
8 large garlic cloves, peeled and
  left whole
¼ cup | 60ml apple cider vinegar
1¼ cups | 300ml vegetable stock
4 sprigs fresh oregano or za'atar
½ recipe of tahini sauce
  (page 32)
2 tbsp chopped fresh parsley
½ tsp Aleppo chile flakes
  (or regular chile flakes)

Heat 2 tablespoons of the olive oil in a large, lidded frying pan over medium-high heat, and sear the cabbage wedges on all sides for 3 minutes, until nicely golden. Season with ½ teaspoon of salt and a good grind of black pepper, then transfer the wedges to a plate and set aside.

Add the rest of the oil and the onions to the same pan and cook for 5 minutes, stirring a couple of times, then add the garlic and vinegar and bring to a boil. Add the stock, a heaping ¼ teaspoon of salt and a good grind of black pepper and bring to a boil again. Return the cabbage wedges to the pan and scatter the oregano sprigs on top. Cover and cook over low heat for 50 minutes, by which time the cabbage should be almost melting.

Spoon the tahini sauce all over the cabbage and place under a hot broiler for 4–5 minutes, making sure you keep an eye on it until the tahini starts to get golden.

Garnish the dish with the chopped parsley, chile flakes and a good drizzle of olive oil.

sharing and special occasions

Palestinians boast a rich cultural tapestry woven with vibrant traditions, spanning music, dance, art and cuisine. Among these, Palestinian culinary delights stand out for their intricate layers of flavor and variety. They reflect centuries-old Arab traditions deeply rooted in the Levant region's historical significance as a vital spiritual and trade hub.

For Palestinians, the connection to the land, farming, seasons and elements is not merely a way of life but rather a profound attachment preserved through generations. This deep-rooted bond with nature permeates their farming practices, culinary traditions and daily rituals, offering glimpses into a lifestyle that resonates with people across the globe.

From rummaniyya, falafel and hummus to m'tabbal, mejadara, malfouf and musaqa'a, these vegan specialities graced Palestinian tables long before the recent surge in popularity of plant-based diets.

Some Palestinian home cooking is about dishes that take a bit more time and attention to prepare, such as slow-cooked stews (tabeekh and yakhani), stuffed vegetables (mahashi), sheet pan recipes (sawani) and fried dishes (makali).

In this chapter, you will discover a selection of these dishes, some quick to prepare and others demanding patience and planning. They are not just recipes but a journey into our past, a testament to the depth, richness, authenticity and value of Palestinian cooking.

Ranging from freekeh-stuffed vegetables, fattet adas, ouzi parcels, eggplant with ful, to maftoul and couscous fritters, some of these dishes require a bit of organizing and planning in advance. Some can be prepared ahead of time and stored in the freezer, and others can happily sit in the fridge for a day or two, ready to be savored over several meals.

Throughout the Middle East and Palestine we love stuffing vegetables, though it has to be said that it is a true labor of love. Some of these dishes take a considerable amount of time to make, yet once they land on the table they vanish in a matter of minutes.

If you can't get Romano peppers, use small regular red and yellow peppers, which are available pretty much all year round and have the sweetness that works perfectly in contrast with the tangy, smoky flavor of the stuffing. You can also use flavorful summer tomatoes as an alternative.

The peppers will taste even better the next day, reheated in a lidded sauté pan for 20 minutes over a medium-low heat. Serve with bread to mop up all the lovely juices.

Freekeh-stuffed peppers

Mahshi Filfil bil Freekeh

½ cup | 100g cracked freekeh
8–10 medium Romano peppers
  or roasting pimentos
  (1 lb 7 oz | 650g)
16 oz | 450g passata
1¼ cups | 300ml water
¼ cup | 60ml olive oil, plus more
  for drizzling
3 tbsp pomegranate molasses
2 garlic cloves, crushed to
  a paste
1¼ tsp dried mint
salt and black pepper
½ a small onion, finely chopped
  (½ cup | 70g)
¾ cup | 15g fresh parsley, finely
  chopped, plus more to finish
⅓ cup | 7g fresh mint leaves, thinly
  shredded, plus more to finish
1 oz | 30g kale leaves,
  finely chopped
½ tsp Aleppo chile flakes
  (or regular chile flakes)
1¼ tsp ground cumin
1 tsp ground coriander
heaping ¼ tsp ground cinnamon
heaping ¼ tsp ground allspice
1½ tbsp lemon juice

Put the freekeh into a fine sieve and rinse well under running water. Transfer to a small saucepan, cover with plenty of cold water, and let soak for 15 minutes.

Using a small knife, make a vertical cut along the length of each pepper, keeping the stem intact, then gently pry them open and scoop out the seeds. Set aside while you make the sauce.

In a medium bowl, whisk together 10½ oz | 300g of the passata, the water, 2 tablespoons of the olive oil, 2 tablespoons of the pomegranate molasses, half the garlic, ¾ teaspoon of the dried mint, 1 teaspoon of salt and a good grind of black pepper. Pour the mixture into a deep 9 x 13-inch | 25 x 35cm baking dish.

Bring the freekeh to a boil over medium heat, skimming off any surface foam, then decrease the heat and cook for 15 minutes, until the freekeh is done but retains a bite. Drain the freekeh and rinse briefly under cold water, then tip into a large bowl. Add the onion, herbs, kale, spices, lemon juice and the rest of the olive oil, garlic, pomegranate molasses and passata. Add 1¼ teaspoons of salt and a good grind of black pepper and give everything a good stir.

Preheat the oven to 425°F.

Fill the peppers with the freekeh mixture, about 2 heaping tablespoons each, and arrange them cut side up in the baking dish, slightly apart. Cover well with foil and roast for 45 minutes.

Increase the temperature to 450°F, remove the foil and roast for a further 30 minutes, until the peppers are soft and the sauce has slightly thickened. Remove from the oven and allow to cool for 20 minutes. Before serving, drizzle with olive oil and garnish with the extra parsley and mint leaves.

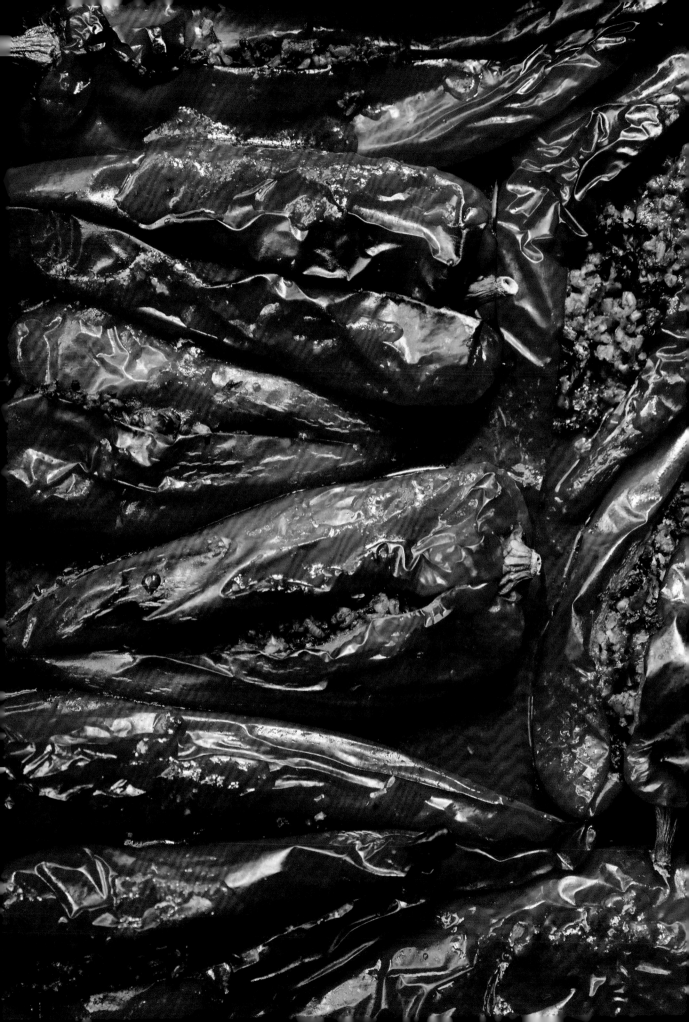

Tomato kubbeh, also known as abu amneh or kamounet banadoura, is a hidden gem of a dish. While less well known than the classic kubbeh, it shares its roots with versions found in parts of Lebanon, Syria and the northern districts of the Golan Heights in Palestine. This is a vegan twist on traditional kubbeh, with a blend of bulgur wheat, tomatoes, mint and kubbeh spice mix.

Abu amneh is a dish that truly shines during the summer months, when tomatoes are at their peak in terms of flavor and freshness. Its light and refreshing nature also makes it a perfect choice for those warm days.

Tomato kubbeh neyeh

Abu Amneh

1 cup | 185g fine bulgur wheat
½ a small onion, finely chopped
   (⅓ cup | 60g)
1 tbsp red pepper paste
   (page 29)
¾ cup | 15g fresh mint leaves
½ tsp dried oregano
2½ tsp baharat (page 39)
1 tsp Aleppo chile flakes
   (or regular chile flakes)
6 large very ripe tomatoes,
   4 cut into quarters and the
   other 2 finely diced
1 tbsp tomato paste
salt
olive oil

To serve
crisp lettuce/cabbage leaves
fresh mint leaves
thinly sliced radishes
chopped onions

Put the bulgur, onion, red pepper paste, mint, herbs and spices into the bowl of a food processor and blitz for 2–3 minutes, until all the ingredients are well incorporated into a fine paste. Add the quartered tomatoes, tomato paste and 1½ teaspoons of salt, and blitz until the tomatoes are very finely chopped, making sure not to overprocess, otherwise the mixture will become too runny. Add the diced tomatoes and mix well.

Transfer the kubbeh to a flat dish, cover and chill for at least 30 minutes. The bulgur at this stage will absorb the tomato juices and become soft.

Spread the kubbeh on a flat serving plate and drizzle generously with olive oil.

Serve with crisp lettuce or cabbage leaves, mint, radishes, onions and good olives in bowls for everyone to help themselves.

The way to eat this is like a taco, wrapping the kubbeh in the leaves, then topping it with the onion, mint and radishes.

Makali means fried or deep-fried vegetables, usually cauliflower, eggplant, potatoes and sometimes tomatoes or zucchini. It's a dish that uses a few simple ingredients, but when stuffed into a warm pita with tahini sauce, it instantly becomes a fulfilling meal.

The vegetables are roasted here, but they can also be fried or cooked on a grill if you prefer. The sandwiches are best eaten warm from the oven; however, if you'd like to prepare them in advance, leave grilling the halloumi until just before serving, as it's best eaten fresh off the grill.

Serves 4

Grilled vegetable sandwiches

Makali

1 small cauliflower, cut into roughly 1½-inch | 4cm florets (12 oz | 350g)
1 small eggplant, sliced into ½-inch | 1½cm rounds (9 oz | 250g)
5 tbsp | 70ml olive oil
1 red onion, cut into ½-inch | 1cm thick slices (1¼ cups | 150g)
salt and black pepper
1 medium zucchini, cut on the diagonal into ½-inch | 1cm thick slices (7 oz | 190g)
2 garlic cloves, crushed to a paste
1 lemon, squeezed to get 1 tbsp juice
½ cup | 10g fresh parsley leaves, roughly chopped
¼ cup | 5g fresh mint leaves, finely shredded
4 pita breads
9 oz | 250g halloumi cheese, cut into ½-inch | 1cm-thick rectangular pieces, 2 x 3 inches | 5 x 7cm
½ tsp Aleppo chile flakes (or regular chile flakes)

To serve
tahini sauce (page 32)
1 lemon, cut into wedges

Preheat the oven to 450°F. Line a baking sheet with parchment paper.

Spread the cauliflower on the prepared baking sheet and set aside.

Place a grill pan over high heat and, once hot, lightly brush the eggplant slices with 2 tablespoons of olive oil and grill them for about 4 minutes, turning them halfway through so that both sides get grill marks. Transfer the eggplant to the baking sheet with the cauliflower. Do the same with the onion.

Drizzle 1 tablespoon of olive oil evenly over the vegetables, season with a heaping ¼ teaspoon of salt and roast for 20–25 minutes, or until the vegetables are golden and tender.

Meanwhile, repeat the process with the zucchini slices, cooking them in the grill pan for 4 minutes, turning them halfway through. Transfer them to a plate, sprinkle with a little salt and set aside.

While the vegetables are roasting, put the garlic and lemon juice into a medium bowl with the herbs, the remaining 2 tablespoons of oil, ½ teaspoon of salt and a good grind of black pepper. Mix to combine and set aside.

Just before serving, place the pita in a low oven or toaster to warm them through. Return the grill pan to high heat. Pat dry the pieces of halloumi and add them to the pan. Grill for 2 minutes, turning them halfway through so that both sides get charred.

Arrange the halloumi on a large serving plate, with the cooked vegetables alongside. Spoon over the garlic dressing and sprinkle with the chile flakes.

Serve with the pita, tahini sauce and lemon wedges, for everyone to make their own sandwich.

The word "fatteh" encompasses a variety of dishes found across the Middle East. Dishes such as fatteh bil hummus and fattet makdous (eggplant fatteh) are celebrated for their ingenious use of stale bread to create flavorful new dishes.

In Palestine, one of our beloved fatteh variations is fatteh adas. This humble dish utilizes simple and affordable ingredients such as lentils, bread and pantry staples (mooneh). It's warm, hearty, comforting and suitable for any mealtime. Personally, I love having it for breakfast the day after it's made, as the flavors meld together beautifully overnight.

Other toppings can be used, such as sumac onions (page 33), black olives, capers, a sprinkle of sumac or crumbled feta cheese. The pistachios can be replaced with other nuts or seeds.

Serves 4 for light lunch or supper

Lentil fatteh

Fattet Adas

¾ cup plus 2 tbsp | 180g split
  red lentils, rinsed and drained
4½ cups | 1100ml water
1 small onion, finely chopped
  (½ cup | 80g)
1½ tsp ground cumin
½ tsp ground turmeric
heaping ¼ tsp ground allspice
heaping ¼ tsp ground cinnamon
salt and black pepper
2 tbsp olive oil, plus more for
  drizzling
green lemon sauce (page 28)
2 naan bread, cut into ¾-inch |
  2cm pieces (9 oz | 250g)

For the garnish
¼ cup | 40g pistachios
2 tbsp roughly chopped
  fresh parsley

Put the lentils into a medium saucepan with the water and bring to a boil, skimming off any foam that appears. Decrease the heat to low. Add the onion, spices, 2 teaspoons of salt and a good grind of black pepper. Simmer for 30 minutes, until the lentils are completely mushy.

Take the pan off the heat, add the olive oil and blitz, using a hand-held immersion blender or a freestanding one, for a couple of minutes or until it's almost smooth. Set aside.

While the lentils are cooking, make the green lemon sauce and set aside.

Preheat the oven to 375°F and line a baking sheet with parchment paper.

Place the pistachio nuts on the prepared baking sheet and toast for about 7 minutes. Once the nuts have cooled down, roughly crush them.

Add the bread to the lentil mixture while it's still hot, along with a couple of teaspoons of the green lemon sauce, and mix well so that the bread is completely coated. Cover the pan and let sit for about an hour, to allow the bread to absorb as much of the liquid as possible.

To serve, spoon the fatteh into a large serving bowl and drizzle with most of the remaining green lemon sauce. Garnish with the pistachios and parsley and finish with a good drizzle of olive oil. Serve the rest of the green lemon sauce on the side, for those who like it extra hot.

Sharing and special occasions

Maftoul, often referred to as Palestinian couscous, is an ancient, uniquely Palestinian ingredient consisting of hand-rolled, fine-cracked wheat coated with flour, water and oil and rolled by hand into small pearls. This labor-intensive process gives maftoul its distinctive texture and flavor. Once the pearls are rolled, they are typically sun-dried to remove excess moisture before being stored and cooked.

Maftoul can be prepared in various ways, including steaming, boiling or simmering in broth. It is commonly used as a base for hearty stews, soups or pilafs, and is often served for special occasions and celebrations, symbolizing hospitality and togetherness within Palestinian culture.

Maftoul is cherished not only for its delicious taste but also for its cultural significance in Palestinian cuisine, representing tradition, heritage and the art of handcrafted cooking.

If okra does not rock your boat, other vegetables such as asparagus, green beans and broccoli can be used instead.

Maftoul with tomato, okra & yogurt

Maftoul bil Banadoura ma' Bamia

6 tbsp | 90ml olive oil
1 large onion, peeled and finely
   sliced (1½ cups | 180g)
5 garlic cloves, peeled and
   crushed to a paste
¾ tsp ground allspice
1 tsp cumin seeds
½ tsp ground cinnamon
14 oz | 400g cherry tomatoes
1 tbsp tomato paste
1⅔ cups | 400ml water
salt and black pepper
9 oz | 250g maftoul, fregola
   or pearl couscous
1 lb 2 oz | 500g fresh or
   frozen okra

To serve
Greek yogurt
¼ cup | 5g fresh mint leaves
1 tbsp sumac

Put ¼ cup | 60ml of oil into a large, lidded sauté pan and place over medium heat. Once hot, fry the onion for 7 minutes, stirring a few times, until caramelized and soft.

Add the garlic, allspice, cumin seeds and cinnamon and fry for a minute, stirring continuously, until fragrant and starting to brown, then add the cherry tomatoes, mashing them with a potato masher to break them up. Stir in the tomato paste, the water, 1 teaspoon of salt and a good grind of black pepper and bring to a boil, turn down the heat to medium-low, then cover and cook for 10 minutes.

Add the maftoul, stirring it in so it's completely coated, then bring to a quick boil, decrease the heat, cover and cook for 5 minutes. Take off the heat and set aside for 15 minutes, so the maftoul can absorb all the liquid.

Meanwhile, preheat the oven to 450°F and line a large baking sheet with parchment paper. Put the okra into a large bowl with 2 tablespoons of oil, ½ teaspoon of salt and a good grind of black pepper. Mix, then spread out on the prepared baking sheet and roast for 15 minutes, stirring once halfway through, until the okra is slightly caramelized and soft. Take it out of the oven and set aside.

Divide the maftoul between four plates and serve with the okra alongside. Add a spoonful of yogurt, scatter some mint leaves on top and finish with a sprinkle of sumac.

There is a whole array of kubbeh or kibbeh out there. It is one of the most prominent Middle Eastern dishes, renowned for its various fillings and casings.

Traditionally, kubbeh is made into croquettes or casseroles, with raw minced lamb or beef mixed with fine bulgur wheat and spices. Other types of kubbeh are vegan, using vegetables such as potato, tomato, pumpkin or, as in this recipe, sweet potato. The filling in this kubbeh is sweet and sharp with onion and sumac.

Kubbeh are super easy to make and can be served as a main dish or as part of a larger spread.

Makes 24 pieces, to serve 12 as a snack or 8 as a main

Sweet potato kubbeh with chile salsa

Kubbet Batata Helweh

For the shell

3–4 sweet potatoes
  (1 lb 9 oz | 700g)
1⅓ cups | 250g coarse
  bulgur wheat
1⅔ cups | 400ml boiling water
1 onion, finely chopped
  (1 cup | 150g)
1½ tsp Aleppo chile flakes
  (or regular chile flakes)
1 tbsp ground cumin
2 tsp ground coriander
2 garlic cloves, crushed to
  a paste
½ tsp dried oregano
1 cup | 20g fresh parsley,
  finely chopped
½ cup | 10g fresh dill,
  finely chopped
3 tbsp olive oil
2 tbsp cornstarch
salt
about 2 cups | 500ml sunflower
  oil, for frying

First make the kubbeh shell. Preheat the oven to 425°F. Wrap the sweet potatoes individually in foil, and place on a baking sheet. Bake for about 50–60 minutes, until completely soft. Allow to cool, scoop out the insides, then mash the flesh and transfer to a large bowl.

While the potatoes are cooking, place the bulgur wheat in a medium bowl and cover with the boiling water. Soak for 15 minutes. Drain well, then tip into a clean kitchen towel, draw the sides up and squeeze out as much water as possible.

Add the soaked bulgur, onion, spices, garlic, herbs, oil, cornstarch and 1¾ teaspoons of salt to the bowl of sweet potato flesh and, using your hands, mix well. Set aside.

To make the filling, heat the olive oil in a large frying pan, then add the onions and cook for 15–18 minutes, stirring often, until they are soft and starting to caramelize. Remove the pan from the heat and add the sumac, lemon juice, ¾ teaspoon of salt and a good grind of black pepper. Mix well and set aside to cool completely.

To form the kubbeh, divide the shell mixture into 24 equal-size balls, weighing about 2¼ oz | 60g each. Have a small bowl of water at hand in case the mixture is a bit sticky.

Working one at a time, take a ball in the palm of one hand, and using the index finger of the opposite hand, form a deep well in the center. Place about 1 tablespoon of the filling in the well, pushing down gently. Pinch the open sides of the shell together, smoothing down as you go, so that the filling is covered with the shell.

Sharing and special occasions

For the filling

2½ tbsp olive oil

3 onions, halved and finely sliced
 (3½ cups | 450g)

4½ tbsp sumac (1½ oz | 40g)

3 tbsp lemon juice

For the chile salsa

2 cups | 40g fresh parsley,
 including stalks, roughly
 chopped

2 cups | 40g fresh cilantro,
 including stalks, roughly
 chopped

1 small green chile, half the seeds
 removed, roughly chopped

7 tbsp | 110ml olive oil

2 tbsp lemon juice

½ tsp granulated sugar

¼ cup | 60ml water

Using both hands, shape the kubbeh into a slightly flattened pattie, about 3 inches | 8cm wide, making sure no cracks appear. Transfer to a baking sheet lined with parchment paper. Repeat until all the shell and filling mixtures are used up. Set aside until you are ready to fry.

Place all the ingredients for the chile salsa in a blender with 1 teaspoon of salt and blitz until you have a smooth paste. Transfer the salsa to a bowl and set aside, or cover and chill if cooking the kubbeh later.

When ready to fry, put the sunflower oil into a 11-inch | 28cm, high-sided frying pan and place over medium-low heat. When the oil is hot (350°F, if you have a thermometer), add the kubbeh in batches of 4 or 5, and fry for 2–2½ minutes each side, until golden brown and crisp. Keep an eye on them—they can color quickly due to the high sugar content of the sweet potato. Remove using a slotted spoon and put them on to a plate lined with paper towels. Keep warm in a preheated oven (350°F) on a lined oven tray while you continue with the remaining kubbeh.

Transfer the kubbeh to a serving platter and serve warm, with the chile salsa to dip them into.

Kubbeh can be prepared a day in advance and kept in the fridge ready for frying. They also freeze well, and can be fried straight from the freezer. To freeze, lay them out on a baking sheet first. Once frozen, transfer them into a sealable bag for storage. They keep in the freezer for up to 2 months.

215

Kubbet hileh translates to "counterfeit kubbeh" in Arabic, as it looks and tastes as it if has meat in it, but it's vegan. It's a simple dish, but that's where its beauty lies. The dish is enjoyed particularly during Lent, throughout Palestine, Lebanon and Syria. Personally, I think it's too good not to be enjoyed for the rest of the year.

The ingenuity of dishes like kubbet hileh is that in each region in the Middle East the same dish takes a slightly different form. In some cases, it might be served as a soup, or the kubbeh balls are served on their own, topped with caramelized onions and sumac. Each version is unique and utterly delicious.

Bulgur kubbeh

Kubbet Hileh

For the kubbeh
1 cup | 200g fine bulgur wheat
2 tbsp olive oil
1½ tsp ground cumin
1 tsp Aleppo chile flakes
   (or regular chile flakes)
salt
1½ tbsp red pepper paste
   (page 29)
1½ cups | 350ml boiling water
½ cup | 2⅓ oz | 65g all-purpose
   flour
1 garlic clove, crushed to a paste

For the sauce
1 large onion (9 oz | 250g),
   finely chopped
¼ cup | 60ml olive oil
1 tbsp red pepper paste (page 29)
2 tbsp lemon juice
1 tsp ground cumin
3 tbsp | 65g pomegranate
   molasses
1 tbsp honey
⅓ cup | 80ml water

To serve
½ cup | 10g fresh parsley leaves
¼ cup | 5g fresh mint leaves
1 red chile, finely sliced
⅓ cup | 35g walnuts (optional)
tahini sauce (page 32)

Mix the bulgur with the oil, spices, 1¼ teaspoons of salt and the red pepper paste. Add the boiling water, then cover the bowl and let soak for at least 20–30 minutes. Add the flour and crushed garlic and mix well with your hands, squeezing until you have a sticky mixture.

Have a bowl of oil next to you (to stop the mixture sticking to your hands) and shape the mixture into 32 smooth balls, about ½ oz | 15g each, rolling them between the palms of your hands. Place them on a plate or baking sheet, then cover and set aside for 30 minutes.

Fry the onion in the oil for 7 minutes, then add 1 teaspoon of salt and the rest of the sauce ingredients and cook for 3 minutes more.

Bring a large saucepan of salted water to a boil and carefully slip in the kubbeh, gently mixing to prevent them sticking. Cook over medium heat for 10 minutes, then drain and add the kubbeh to the sauce, stirring carefully so they are covered.

Serve from the pan, scattering over the herbs, chile and walnuts (if using), with the tahini sauce on the side.

I'm a total sucker for anything wrapped in pastry, and as a true Arab, I'm obsessed with bread and savory pastries. This dish is a showstopper and will definitely impress your guests. Serve it as part of a brunch or a light lunch, with a few nice salads.

   If asparagus is not in season, the galette works beautifully with broccolini as a substitute.

Asparagus, leek & hazelnut galette

Fattiret Halyoun

For the crust
2 cups | 9 oz | 240g all-purpose flour
salt and black pepper
10 tbsp | 130g unsalted butter, chilled and cut into ½-inch | 1cm cubes
⅓ cup | 90g Greek yogurt
2 tsp apple cider vinegar
1½ tbsp ice water

For the filling
¼ cup | 60ml olive oil
2 leeks, white and light green parts only, trimmed and sliced into ½-inch | 1cm slices (7 oz | 200g)
6 oz | 180g soft goat cheese (heaping 1 cup crumbled)
3 oz | 80g cheddar cheese, grated (¾ cup | 90g)
2 garlic cloves, crushed to a paste
1½ tsp lemon zest
1½ tbsp fresh za'atar or oregano leaves, finely chopped
9 oz | 250g asparagus, woody ends trimmed
2 tbsp za'atar
1 egg yolk, beaten with 1 tbsp water, to glaze
3 tbsp | 25g hazelnuts, lightly toasted and roughly chopped

For the crust, put the flour into the bowl of a food processor with a heaping ¼ teaspoon of salt and ⅛ teaspoon of black pepper and pulse to combine. Add the butter and pulse for 2–3 minutes until the texture is like wet sand, with the biggest pieces of butter being the size of small pebbles.

Add the yogurt, vinegar and ice water and pulse just until the dough comes together. Shape the dough into a ball, then wrap it in parchment paper and chill it for at least 1 hour and up to 2 days.

Heat 1 tablespoon of the olive oil in a medium pan, then add the leeks and cook over medium heat for 5 minutes, until the leeks start to caramelize and soften. Season with a heaping ¼ teaspoon salt and a grind of black pepper.

In a medium bowl, mix the goat cheese with ¼ cup | 30g of the cheddar cheese, the garlic, lemon zest, fresh za'atar or oregano leaves and a heaping ¼ teaspoon of salt, until you have a spreadable consistency.

Toss the asparagus with 1 tablespoon of olive oil, ½ tablespoon of za'atar, a heaping ¼ teaspoon of salt and a good grind of black pepper.

Place the remaining 2 tablespoons of oil and the rest of the za'atar in a small bowl, stir well and set aside.

Place the dough on a well-floured sheet of parchment paper (about 20 inches | 50cm square) and roll out to form a rough circle. It will have uneven edges, but should measure about 16 inches | 40cm wide. Lifting up both the parchment and the dough, transfer to a large rimless baking sheet and put it into the fridge to rest for 30 minutes.

Take the dough out of the fridge and spread with the goat cheese mixture, leaving a border of about 1 inch / 2½cm around the edge. Sprinkle with the remaining ½ cup / 50g of cheddar, and top with the leeks, spreading them out evenly (avoid crowding them too much in the middle, or the pie crust won't cook properly).

Arrange the asparagus evenly on top of the leeks, slightly overlapping so that the cheese and leeks are covered. Fold the border over the filling, pleating it as necessary, leaving the center open. Refrigerate the gallete for 20 minutes or up to 6 hours.

Heat the oven to 425°F.

Brush the edges of the galette with the egg/water mixture and bake for 35 minutes, until it is golden brown and the bottom is cooked through. Remove the galette from the oven and leave it to rest for 5 minutes. Before serving, spoon over the za'atar oil and sprinkle the hazelnuts over the top.

This dish was inspired by my mum's couscous with tomato and onion. This recipe is not only a testament to its easy and quick preparation, but also a clever way to revitalize leftover couscous. With just a simple mix of ingredients, your couscous becomes lovely fritters, pan-fried to golden perfection. These wonderfully comforting crunchy fritters are served with zesty preserved lemon yogurt.

For a vegan version, simply replace the egg with an additional 1–2 tablespoons of cornstarch, though the fritters will have a slightly more delicate and crumbly texture than the egg-based version.

Couscous fritters with preserved lemon yogurt

Aqras Kosukson

2 tbsp olive oil
1 medium onion, finely chopped
  (1¼ cups | 160g)
1 tbsp tomato paste
1 tbsp red pepper paste (page 29)
1 red bell pepper, finely chopped
  (7 oz | 200g)
4 very ripe tomatoes, cut into
  ¼-inch | ½cm dice (12 oz | 350g)
3 medium carrots, peeled and
  coarsely grated (1⅔ cups | 185g)
5¼ oz | 150g couscous
1 cup | 220ml boiling
  vegetable stock
1 egg
¼ cup | 34g cornstarch
1 tbsp lemon zest
¼ cup | 60ml sunflower oil, for frying

For the preserved lemon yogurt
½ cup | 150g Greek yogurt
1 tbsp preserved lemon,
  finely chopped
1 tbsp capers, finely chopped
1 tbsp fresh dill, finely chopped
1 tsp fresh mint leaves, finely
  shredded
salt and black pepper

Start by making the preserved lemon yogurt: put all the ingredients into a medium bowl, along with ¾ teaspoon of salt and a grind of black pepper. Whisk well, then cover and store in the fridge until needed.

Pour the olive oil into a 12-inch | 30cm sauté pan and place it over medium heat. Add the onion and cook for 5 minutes, stirring often, until it has softened but not colored. Stir in the tomato paste and red pepper paste and cook for 1 minute. Add the red pepper, tomatoes, 1 teaspoon of salt and a good grind of black pepper and cook for 3 minutes. Add the carrots and cook for another 3 minutes.

Add the couscous to the pan and stir well. Add the hot stock and stir again, then cover the pan. Lower the heat and allow to cook for 10–12 minutes, until all the liquid has been absorbed and the couscous has softened and swelled.

Remove from the heat and allow to cool. Add the egg, cornstarch and lemon zest and mix well. Form into 12–13 patties (2¼ oz | 60g each), about 2½ inches | 6cm wide and 1¼ inches | 3cm thick.

Heat the oven to 400°F and line a baking sheet with parchment paper. Heat the sunflower oil in a large nonstick frying | sauté pan over medium-high heat and cook the patties for 3 minutes on each side, until golden. Place on the prepared baking sheet and cook in the oven for a further 5 minutes, until piping hot inside.

Serve warm, with the preserved lemon yogurt and a salad.

This Palestinian celebratory dish is believed to be originally from Damascus, in Syria. It's a splendid rice dish with the right balance of seasoning that works well with the meatiness of the cremini mushrooms, the sweetness of the vegetables/golden raisins and the crunch of the toasted nuts and seeds.

The main and nicest part of ouzi is the rice, cooked with diced carrots, peas and spices. Serve with a chopped salad (page 80), or with tahini, tomato & mint dip (page 92).

Ouzi phyllo parcels

Ouzi

⅔ cup | 120g Egyptian or other
    short-grain rice
salt
¾ cup | 160g orzo
5 tbsp | 75ml olive oil
1 medium onion, finely chopped
    (1¼ cups | 175g)
9 oz | 250g cremini mushrooms,
    cut into quarters
1¾ tsp ground allspice
¾ tsp ground cinnamon
½ tsp ground cardamom
⅓ tsp ground black pepper
½ tsp ground turmeric
6 large garlic cloves, thinly sliced
12¼ oz | 350g carrots, 3½ oz | 100g
    coarsely grated (a heaping
    ¾ cup), the rest cut into
    ¼-inch | ½cm dice
3 cups | 700ml vegetable stock
1 cup | 150g frozen peas, thawed
¾ cup | 100g golden or regular
    raisins
¾ cup | 100g toasted nuts and
    seeds (page 35)
6 tbsp | 85g unsalted butter,
    melted
15 (12 x 15-inch | 30 x 38cm)
    sheets of good-quality
    phyllo pastry, thawed

For the garnish
¼ cup | 5g parsley leaves
1 tbsp olive oil
sumac

Rinse the rice, put it into a bowl and cover with plenty of cold water. Add ½ teaspoon of salt and set aside to soak.

Heat a large saucepan, one which has a lid, then add the orzo and cook over medium heat for 5 minutes, stirring a few times, until it's golden. Remove the orzo from the pan and set aside.

Add 3 tablespoons of olive oil and the onion to the same pan and cook over medium-low heat for 5 minutes. Increase the heat to medium, add the mushrooms and cook for 5 minutes, until the mushrooms are soft. Add the spices and a heaping ¼ teaspoon of salt, mix well, then transfer the mixture to a bowl and set aside.

Add the remaining olive oil to the pan with the garlic and cook for 1 minute, then add the grated and diced carrots and cook for 2 minutes more. Stir in the rice and orzo, then add the stock and 1¼ teaspoons of salt and bring to a boil. Wrap the pot lid in a clean kitchen towel and pop it on top. Decrease the heat and cook for 15 minutes, then take the pot off the heat. Spread the rice out onto a large oven tray and set aside to cool down for 20 minutes. When the rice has cooled down slightly, stir in the peas, golden raisins and ⅓ cup | 40g of nuts and seeds.

Brush a 2 inch deep x 5 inch wide | 5 x 12cm soup bowl with melted butter and set aside. Lay the sheets of phyllo pastry on a surface and cut them in half widthways. Brush each pastry half with melted butter, then layer them in the bowl so that the base is covered and the phyllo rises up and over the bowl's sides. Repeat with the next sheet of phyllo, brushing first with butter, then arranging it in the bowl, rotating it slightly so that the excess hangs at different angle. Repeat this process, brushing each piece with butter as you go, until you have used up 5 pieces of phyllo in total and the base and the sides are all covered.

Next, spoon about 1½ cups | 280g of your prepared rice mixture into the center of the pastry. Fold the overhanging pastry edges over the filling to close the parcel, brushing the folds with butter to hold them in place. Carefully tip the parcel on to a lined baking tray. Repeat the process to make a total of 6 parcels.

Bake the parcels in the preheated oven at 400°F for 25 minutes. Increase the temperature to 425°F and bake for a further 10 minutes, until the parcels are deeply golden. Let them cool slightly before serving.

Add the remaining nuts and seeds to a medium bowl with the parsley and olive oil, and mix well. Divide and place the mixture on top of all the parcels, before sprinkling with sumac and serving.

Fatteh is one of those dishes that each household makes slightly differently. It's a centerpiece, placed in the middle of the table for everyone to tuck into. It is a dish to fall in love with and to make over and over again.

Fatteh makdous must strike a balance between the crunchiness of the bread, the tartness of the tomato sauce and the creaminess of the yogurt tahini. It's what you want from such a star dish.

All the components for the fatteh can be made a day or so in advance and assembled just before serving. To make this vegan, leave out the yogurt and make tahini sauce instead (page 32).

Roasted eggplant fatteh

Fattet Makdous

2 pita breads or 4 large flour tortillas, cut into ¾–1¼ inch | 2–3cm pieces (8½ oz | 240g)
5 tbsp | 70ml olive oil, plus more for drizzling
2 medium eggplants, cut into 1¼-inch | 3cm chunks (1 lb 2 oz | 500g)
2 tsp sumac
½ tsp sweet paprika
salt and black pepper

For the yogurt sauce
2 cups | 400g Greek yogurt
3 tbsp tahini paste
1 garlic clove, crushed to a paste
1 green chile, finely chopped
2 tbsp lemon juice

For the tomato sauce
1 medium onion, finely chopped (1¼ cups | 175g)
2 tbsp olive oil
16 oz | 450g passata
1 tbsp pomegranate molasses

To serve
¼ cup | 35g whole blanched almonds, toasted
¼ cup | 5g fresh parsley, roughly chopped
1 red chile, finely chopped
3 tbsp | 30g pomegranate seeds (optional)

Preheat the oven to 400°F and line a baking sheet with parchment paper.

Put the bread pieces into a bowl with 2½ tbsp | 35ml of the olive oil and mix well to coat. Lay the bread in one layer on the prepared baking sheet and bake for 17 minutes, or until golden and crispy. Leave aside for later.

Increase the oven temperature to 450°F. Put the eggplant chunks into a large bowl, add the remaining 2½ tbsp | 35ml of olive oil, the sumac, paprika, ½ teaspoon of salt and a good grind of black pepper and toss well to coat. Arrange the eggplant on a parchment-lined baking sheet and roast for 25 minutes, or until golden and cooked through.

While the eggplant is cooking, make the yogurt sauce. Put all the ingredients into a medium bowl, add ½ teaspoon of salt and mix well to combine. Store in the fridge until needed.

To make the tomato sauce, put the onion into a small saucepan with the olive oil and cook over medium-low heat for 10 minutes, or until the onion is golden and soft. Add the passata, pomegranate molasses, a heaping ¼ teaspoon of salt and a good grind of black pepper. Bring to a gentle boil and simmer on a very low heat for 7 minutes, until the sauce has thickened.

When ready to serve, layer the bread pieces at the bottom of a serving platter with a lip or a wide shallow bowl. Spoon over the yogurt sauce, followed by the tomato sauce. Arrange the eggplant chunks on top and garnish with the almonds, parsley, chile and pomegranate seeds, if using, then finish with a drizzle of olive oil.

bread

Bread holds a significant cultural, social and economic importance for Palestinians, as it does in many cultures around the world. In Palestine, bread is often seen as a symbol of sustenance and hospitality. Sharing bread with others is a way of showing generosity, a heartfelt welcome into the home of every Palestinian family.

No meal is complete without the blessing of freshly baked bread. It complements dishes and is used as a tool in different ways—for scooping, mopping, dipping or dunking. Sharing bread is a gesture of warmth, emphasizing the communal nature of meals in Palestinian culture and enforcing the importance of unity and tradition.

The Middle East boasts a diverse array of bread: taboon, khubez, pita, ka'ak, manakish, markook, fatayer and kemaj, to name just a few.

Other types of Palestinian bread fall into the category of moajanat, which refers to a variety of Palestinian savory and sweet pastries that are enjoyed as snacks or desserts. These pastries come in different shapes and with different fillings, showcasing regionality and seasonality. Common savory varieties include ingredients such as cheese, spinach, fresh za'atar or meat, and sweet options are filled with nuts, dates or sweetened cheeses.

Nowadays people prefer to get their khubez, markook and Jerusalem's sesame ka'ak from trusted local bakeries, while moajanat varieties are typically homemade.

Steeped in history, ka'ak al quds—Jerusalem sesame bread—offers a delightful blend of tradition and simplicity. Requiring only basic pantry ingredients, these adorable nests are ideal for a picnic or served as part of any meal. Once baked, these comforting treats can be savored with a variety of accompaniments, such as za'atar, labneh, cream cheese, or simply butter and jam. Indulge in their timeless appeal and savor a taste of history with every bite.

Buying ka'ak in Jerusalem is not just a transaction, it's an experience that encapsulates the essence of tradition and local flavors. Alongside the freshly baked bread comes hamim—oven-baked eggs—a small sachet of za'atar and salt, inviting a culinary journey through the streets of Jerusalem. This ritual isn't just about satisfying hunger; it's about connecting to one's cultural roots and hometown. Each bite becomes a nostalgic embrace, weaving memories and heritage into a timeless recipe that holds a special place in the heart of those who cherish it.

Jerusalem sesame bread nests

Ka'ak al Quds ma' Beyd

2¼ tsp | 7g fast-acting (instant) dried yeast
1½ tbsp granulated sugar
1¼ cups | 300ml lukewarm water
4 cups | 1 lb 2 oz | 500g all-purpose flour, plus more for dusting
1½ tsp mahlab
1 tsp anise seeds, slightly crushed
salt
3 tbsp sunflower oil, plus more for greasing
9 medium eggs
3 tbsp white sesame seeds
2 tbsp black sesame seeds

Put the yeast, sugar and water into a small bowl. Whisk together well, then set aside for 5 minutes, until the mixture has frothed.

Place the flour, mahlab, anise seeds and 1¾ teaspoons of salt in the bowl of a stand mixer with a dough hook in place. Whisk the ingredients together, then add the sunflower oil and the yeast mixture, and mix on medium speed for 3 minutes, until the dough comes together. Remove the dough from the bowl and gently shape into a ball on greased surface, then rub lightly all over with sunflower oil. Return it to the bowl, cover, and set aside in a warm place for 1 to 1½ hours, or until it has doubled in size.

When the dough is ready, tip it on to a lightly floured clean surface and divide it into 8 pieces, about 3½ oz | 110g each. Shape each piece into a ball, tucking the dough under the base. Cover with a clean kitchen towel and leave to rest for 10 minutes.

Lightly flour your hands. Dig your finger into the center of one of the dough balls, to create a hole, then slightly stretch the dough outwards to create a ring. Repeat this for all the dough balls and then arrange the dough rings on to 2 large parchment-lined baking sheets, leaving lots of space between them.

Whisk one of the eggs in a small bowl and brush all over the rings, then sprinkle with the white and black sesame seeds. Tuck an egg in the center of each ring, making sure the eggs are placed on their side. Cover again and leave for at least 20 minutes.

Adjust the oven racks to the upper- and lower-middle positions and preheat the oven to 425°F. Place a small baking dish or metal loaf pan in the bottom of the oven and pour about 1¼ cups / 300ml of boiling water into it.

Bake the bread for 20–22 minutes, switching and rotating the baking sheets halfway through baking, or until golden brown. Remove from the oven and allow the bread to cool slightly before serving.

Serve with olive oil and za'atar for dipping.

"Kubez" bread, also known as kimaaj, is Arabic flatbread or pita bread. It is a staple in the Middle East, and is used as a versatile accompaniment for various dishes or as a wrap for sandwiches.

Kubez is typically round and flat, with a soft and chewy texture. The dough is rolled out into thin rounds and baked at a high temperature, causing it to puff up and create a pocket inside, perfect for stuffing with vegetables, spreads or dips.

I've used 100% all-purpose flour for this recipe, but feel free to experiment with a blend of all-purpose and whole-wheat flour if you prefer. The results will be equally fantastic.

This bread can also be stored and reheated later, either by wrapping it in foil and warming it in the oven or by quickly toasting it under the broiler or on the stovetop.

Pan-fried turmeric bread

Kubez Kimaaj

1½ tsp fast-acting (instant) dried yeast
1 tbsp granulated sugar
¾ cup plus 2 tbsp | 200ml lukewarm water
3 cups | 13 oz | 370g all-purpose flour
heaping ¼ tsp ground turmeric
2 tbsp sunflower oil, plus more for greasing
salt

Put the yeast, sugar and water into a small bowl and set aside for 5 minutes, or until the mixture starts to bubble.

Put the flour, turmeric, sunflower oil and 1 teaspoon of salt into the bowl of a stand mixer with the dough hook attachment in place. Mix on a low speed for 1 minute, just to combine, then add the yeast mixture. Work on low speed for 2 minutes to bring everything together, then increase the speed to medium and continue to mix for 3 minutes, until the dough is soft and elastic.

Tip the dough on to a clean work surface and bring together to form a ball. Grease the bowl with a bit of oil, then return the dough to the bowl. Turn it a couple of times so that it's completely coated in the oil, then cover the bowl with a clean kitchen towel and let rest somewhere warm for 1 to 1½ hours, or until the dough has doubled in size.

Cut the dough into 8 equal pieces (2½ oz | 70g each) and roll each out into a 6-inch | 15cm circle. After all the pieces are rolled out, cover them with a slightly damp kitchen towel and let them rest again for 20 minutes.

Place a large nonstick frying pan over medium heat, and when hot, dry-fry the bread for about 6 minutes, turning a few times to help the bread puff up. Put the cooked bread onto a large kitchen towel, well spaced out, while you repeat the same with the rest of the dough circles. Place another kitchen towel over the cooked bread and leave it to cool down slightly, to keep the bread moist and pillowy.

Serve warm, or wrap well and store in the freezer.

Fenugreek, known as helbeh, is a versatile herb in Palestine, with diverse culinary uses. Its seeds serve as a flavorful spice, and are often toasted or fried to intensify their flavor. Conversely, the fenugreek leaves are used as a vibrant, fresh, green herb, enhancing soups, stews, breads and pastries. Fenugreek is also enjoyed as a tea, which is brewed from the seeds or leaves and is prized for its digestive properties, for supporting lactation during pregnancy and for its overall wellness benefits.

These buns are delicious and fragrant—they are made with fenugreek seeds, mint and sweet caramelized onions.

Fenugreek & onion buns

Aqras Helbeh

For the buns
1½ tsp fast-acting (instant) dried yeast
1½ tsp granulated sugar
¾ cup plus 2 tbsp | 200ml lukewarm water
3 cups | 13 oz | 370g all-purpose flour, plus more for dusting
salt and black pepper
3 tbsp sunflower oil
1 tbsp olive oil

For the filling
3 tbsp olive oil
2 large onions, finely chopped (2⅔ cups | 370g)
3 tbsp | 40g fenugreek seeds, soaked overnight in plenty of water
2 tsp ground cumin
¾ tsp ground turmeric
1 tbsp dried mint
7 oz | 200g feta cheese, crumbled (1½ cups) (optional)

Whisk together the yeast, sugar and water in a bowl and set aside for 5 minutes, until it starts to bubble.

Sift the flour and 1 teaspoon of salt into the bowl of a stand mixer with the dough hook in place. Add the yeast mixture and the sunflower oil. Work on a low speed for a few minutes, to bring everything together, then increase the speed to medium-high. Continue to mix for 5–6 minutes, until the dough is soft and elastic. Cover the bowl with a clean kitchen towel and set aside somewhere warm for half an hour, until the dough is slightly risen.

Meanwhile, for the filling, put the olive oil into a large sauté pan and place over medium heat. Add the onions and fry for 7 to 15 minutes, stirring frequently, until the onions are soft and have taken on a bit of color. Add the drained fenugreek seeds, spices, dried mint, 1 teaspoon of salt and a good grind of black pepper, and cook for a further 3 minutes. Remove from the heat and set aside for the mix to cool down completely.

Brush a rimmed baking sheet lightly with olive oil, line with parchment paper and set aside.

Transfer the dough to a lightly floured work surface. Flatten the dough, then roll into a rectangle about 19 x 16 inches | 50 x 40cm and 1/16–⅛-inch | 2–3mm thick. Dust with a little flour if you need to, to prevent the dough sticking to your work surface.

Spread the onion mixture, and the feta, if using, all over the dough, taking it right up to the edges. With the long edge facing toward you, carefully roll up the dough as you would a jelly roll, gently

For the parsley oil

3 tbsp olive oil

½ cup | 10g fresh parsley, finely chopped

1 large garlic clove, crushed to a paste

pressing the roll to make sure there are no air pockets. Trim about ¾ inch | 2cm off both ends and cut the roll into 20 equal pieces, about 1 inch | 3cm long.

Arrange the pieces on the prepared baking sheet, evenly spaced apart and cut side up, so that the filling is showing. Cover the pan with a slightly damp kitchen towel and leave to rise in a warm place for about 1 hour.

About 15 minutes before the hour is up, preheat the oven to 425°F. Bake the buns for 25 to 30 minutes, until they are cooked through and golden brown, then cover loosely with foil and cook for another 10 minutes, or until they are cooked through.

Remove from the oven and set aside to cool down for 30 minutes while you mix all the ingredients for the parsley oil in a small bowl. Once the buns have cooled, brush the oil evenly over the top of them and serve.

Malatit, or qaraquish, as they're also called, are a favorite staple in Palestinian kitchens, available in both sweet and savory variations. These delicious crispy textured crackers are a creative way to utilize leftover dough, by adding seeds, spices and sugar to produce a versatile biscuit-like treat. Perfect for cheeseboards and snacking but also great to give to children. I fondly recall how my mum would divide the uneven edges of the malatit between me and my siblings to have with warm oversweetened mint tea.

Za'atar & anise crackers

Malatit

¼ cup | 30g white sesame seeds
1 tbsp nigella seeds
2 cups | 9 oz | 250g all-purpose flour
2 tbsp za'atar
1 tbsp ground anise seed
1 tsp Aleppo chile flakes (or regular chile flakes)
heaping ¼ tsp mahlab
1½ tsp baking powder
1 tbsp granulated sugar
salt
3 tbsp | 45ml olive oil
3 tbsp | 50ml sunflower oil
about 7 tbsp | 100ml lukewarm water

Adjust the racks to the middle and lower positions and heat the oven to 400°F.

Place the sesame and nigella seeds in a small pan and toast for 3 minutes over medium-low heat. Set aside to cool down.

Put the cooled seeds into a bowl with the flour, spices, baking powder, sugar and 1¼ teaspoons of salt and mix well to combine, then add the oils and mix until the dough comes together.

Gradually (not all in one go) add the water and mix to combine until you get a slightly sticky but elastic dough. Cover the bowl with a plate and let rest at room temperature for 10 minutes.

Divide the dough into two equal pieces. Place one piece of dough between two large sheets of parchment paper and roll it with a rolling pin until it's ⅛-inch | 3–4mm thick—you are looking for a rectangle about 10 x 14 inches | 25 x 35cm. Transfer the dough to a large baking sheet and carefully peel away the top layer of parchment paper.

Cut the dough into 2-inch | 5cm squares or diamond-shaped pieces. The crackers can be also cut into circles, using a 3-inch | 7cm cookie cutter. Repeat the process with the second piece of dough. Bake for about 15 minutes, switching and rotating the baking sheets halfway through baking, until the top is golden.

Allow to cool down completely before serving.

The crackers can be stored in an airtight container for up to a week, maintaining their crispiness and flavor. Alternatively, they can be stored in the freezer for up to a month.

Musafan bread is a great addition to any breakfast or brunch spread. The pillowy layers of bread, oozing with jam and cheese, reveal their deliciousness with each slice.

Here I'm using similar dough to that used for the cheese and sumac bites (page 265), with minor adjustments. It creates the perfect base for this treat. If you want to get ahead, you can prepare the dough a day in advance and store it in the fridge. Bring it to room temperature before rolling, stuffing and baking.

Serves 6–8

Cheese and jam pie

Musafan

1½ tsp fast-acting (instant) dried yeast

1½ tsp granulated sugar

¾ cup plus 1 tbsp | 190ml lukewarm water

2½ cups | 11¼ oz | 320g all-purpose flour, plus more for dusting

1 tbsp milk powder (optional)

1 tbsp sweet baharat (page 38)

1 tsp ground turmeric

2 tbsp za'atar

salt

2 tbsp | 30ml olive oil, plus more for greasing

1 egg

2 tbsp milk or water

1 tbsp white sesame seeds

1½ tsp nigella seeds

For the filling

⅔ cup | 200g strawberry jam, or any flavor of jam you like

6 oz | 170g feta cheese, crumbled (1¼ cups)

First, make the dough. Put the yeast, sugar and water into a small bowl and whisk to combine. Set aside for 5 minutes, until the mixture has frothed.

Put the flour, milk powder, sweet baharat, turmeric, za'atar and ¾ teaspoon of salt into the bowl of a stand mixer with the dough hook in place. Mix for 1 minute, just to combine, then add the yeast mixture and the oil. Work on a low speed for about 2 minutes, to bring everything together, then increase the speed to medium. Continue to mix for 4 minutes, until the dough is soft and elastic. It should feel very soft and almost sticky, but this is how it should be.

Tip the dough on to a clean work surface and bring together to form a ball. Grease the bowl with 1 tablespoon of oil and return the dough to the bowl. Turn it a couple of times so that it's completely coated in oil, then cover the bowl with a clean kitchen towel. Set aside somewhere warm for 1 to 1½ hours, until it's doubled in size.

On a lightly floured work surface, roll the dough into a large circle, about 18 inches | 45cm in diameter. Spread the jam over evenly, leaving about ¾ inch | 2cm clear at the edge. Sprinkle the feta on top, then fold one side of the dough inward about 4 inches | 10cm. Repeat the process with the rest of the dough edges—you are looking for 6–8 folds in total (the pie should be a 6–8-sided shape). Pinch the center and the open side folds tightly together to seal. Transfer the pie to a parchment-lined baking sheet, cover with a clean kitchen towel and let rest for 20 minutes.

Preheat the oven to 425°F.

In a small bowl, whisk the egg with the milk or water and egg-wash the pie all over. Sprinkle with the sesame and nigella seeds. Set aside to rest for 5 minutes, then bake for about 20 minutes, or until the pie is cooked through and the bottom is golden brown. Remove from the oven and let cool for 10 minutes before serving.

Once baked, the pie keeps well for a few days and freezes beautifully—you can warm it in the oven straight from the freezer.

This recipe draws inspiration from traditional Palestinian bread, which uses fresh za'atar leaves and often cheese. The dough is normally rolled paper-thin and stuffed with za'atar leaves and a mixture of onion, sumac and cheese. After stuffing, the dough is folded into an envelope shape, then fried or baked.

In this recipe, I have substituted fresh za'atar with oregano, as it's easier to find, and have turned it into a loaf, which is dead easy to make. I like serving it in chunky slices while it's warm, or slightly toasted, with a generous spread of butter or, even better, a bowl of olive oil and some za'atar to dip chunks of the bread into.

Oregano & cheese loaf

Kubez al Jeben w al Za'atar

2 cups plus 2 tbsp | 9½ oz | 270g
    all-purpose flour
2 tsp baking powder
½ tsp baking soda
1 tsp mahlab
salt
5½ tsp | 15g sesame seeds
2 tsp nigella seeds
2 medium eggs
1 cup | 260ml milk
¼ cup | 60ml olive oil
1 cup | 30g fresh oregano leaves
3½ oz | 100g feta cheese,
    roughly crumbled (¾ cup)
1¾ oz | 50g halloumi cheese,
    roughly chopped (⅓ cup)

Preheat the oven to 400°F. Line a 4½ x 8½-inch | 10 x 20cm loaf pan with parchment paper and set aside.

Put all the dry ingredients into a large bowl, including 1¼ teaspoons of salt, 1 tablespoon of the sesame seeds and 1½ teaspoons of the nigella seeds, and mix well to combine. In another bowl, whisk the eggs, milk and olive oil together and add to the dry ingredients. Add the oregano leaves and cheese, then, using a spatula, fold gently to combine, making sure not to overmix.

Tip the mixture into the prepared pan and level out with the back of the spatula. Sprinkle with the rest of the sesame and nigella seeds and bake for 30–40 minutes, until the top and sides are golden brown and cooked through.

Allow the bread to cool for 15 minutes in the pan before turning it out and allow to cool for a further 10 minutes before serving.

Once cooled, the bread is great for keeping in the freezer—simply cut the loaf into thick slices, wrap it tightly, and freeze for future use, making it a convenient and delicious option to have on hand.

This is another version of the pan-fried turmeric bread (page 241), but with the use of whole-wheat bread flour, which makes a robust and yet delicious bread with or without the addition of oregano. This bread is on rotation in my house and is a good choice for freezing.

The milk powder gives the bread that extra softness needed with this type of bread, but it can be left out if you are making it for vegans.

Whole-wheat bread

Kubez Asmar

2½ cups | 8¾ oz | 250g
   whole-wheat flour
⅔ cup | 2¾ oz | 80g all-purpose
   flour, plus more for dusting
1 tsp fast-acting (instant)
   dried yeast
1½ tsp granulated sugar
2 tbsp milk powder, optional
salt
¼ cup | 60ml olive oil, plus
   more for greasing
⅔ cup | 12g fresh oregano or
   za'atar leaves (optional)
¾ cup | 180ml lukewarm water

Combine the flours, yeast, sugar, milk powder (if using), and 1 teaspoon of salt in the bowl of a stand mixer with the dough hook in place. (If you don't have a mixer, you can knead the dough by hand; it will take about 10 minutes.) Mix on medium speed for 1 minute, to incorporate the ingredients, then add the oil and the oregano or za'atar, if using. Gradually add the water and mix for 7 minutes, until the dough has come together. Gently shape the dough into an elastic, smooth ball and transfer it to a lightly oiled bowl, then cover with a clean kitchen towel and set aside in a warm place for 1–1½ hours, or until doubled in size.

When the dough has risen, punch it back down and divide it into 8 pieces, about 2⅔ oz | 75g each. Shape each one into a ball, then cover with a slightly damp kitchen towel and let rest for 15 minutes. Working on a lightly floured work surface, roll each ball into a 5½-inch | 14cm wide circle. Place the rolled circles on a floured surface and cover with a kitchen towel for 20 minutes.

Adjust the oven racks to the middle and lower positions and preheat the oven to 500°F. Place two baking sheets in the oven to heat up. When ready to bake, working quickly, remove the hot baking sheets from the oven, line with parchment paper, and place 4 of the circles on each baking sheet, placing well apart, and bake for 4–6 minutes, switching and rotating the baking sheets halfway through once the pitas have puffed, until the breads are puffed up and golden brown.

Arrange the cooked flatbreads on a kitchen towel and keep them covered for 10 minutes, to prevent them drying out. When they have cooled down, you can store them in a sealable bag in a cool place for a few days, or they can be wrapped and stored in the freezer for up to a month.

Using stale bread showcases the resourcefulness and creativity of Palestinian cooking in a way that creates delicious and inventive dishes that help to reduce food waste. Palestinians are champions when it comes to stale bread. Bread that's a few days old can be transformed into various flavorful dishes, such as fattoush, a refreshing salad made with toasted or fried pieces of bread or fattet hummus, a layered dish of warm chickpeas, yogurt and crispy bread. It can be toasted or fried to achieve crispy, crunchy elements in many savory or sweet recipes.

In the same way, stale bread is used to thicken soups and stews, adding body and richness. It absorbs the flavors of the broth, creating a hearty and satisfying meal.

Mumalah, which means salted, is another popular way to utilize stale bread in Palestinian cuisine. The scrumptious pieces of toasted bread are topped with tomato salsa and salted grapes, making them an ideal appetizer or part of a spread.

Toasted bread with tomato & sour grapes

Mumalah

4 stale whole-grain pita breads (8½ oz | 240g)
12 oz | 370g black grapes
¼ cup | 60ml olive oil
salt and black pepper
1 onion, finely chopped (1 cup | 150g)
2 medium ripe tomatoes, finely chopped (8½ oz | 240g)
1 tbsp sumac
2 tbsp apple cider vinegar

For the garnish
½ small red onion, very thinly sliced (⅓ cup | 40g)
½ cup | 10g fresh parsley leaves
1 tsp sumac
1 tbsp olive oil
flaked sea salt

Adjust the oven racks to the upper- and lower-middle positions and preheat the oven to 400°F. Line two baking sheets with parchment paper.

Using a small serrated knife, slice the pita breads open to create two separate rounds.

Arrange the bread pieces on the prepared baking sheets, well apart, and set aside.

Put the grapes into a small bowl and add 1 tablespoon of the olive oil and a heaping ¼ teaspoon of salt. Mix to coat, then transfer to a parchment-lined baking dish and roast for 15 minutes, or until the grapes are slightly golden.

Put the onion, tomatoes, sumac, vinegar and the rest of the oil into a medium bowl. Add ½ teaspoon of salt and a good grind of black pepper and mix well. Spoon the tomato mixture on top of the bread, about 1½–2 tablespoons each, spreading it to cover as much of the bread as you can.

Scatter about 5 or 6 grapes (7 or 8 if they are small) on top and spoon over any of the juice too.

Bake for 25 minutes, until the edges of the bread are golden and slightly crispy.

Meanwhile, make the garnish. Gently mix together the red onion, parsley, sumac and olive oil. When the breads are ready, garnish with the salad and add a couple of pinches of flaked sea salt.

Abu Ali Sinina's is an unassuming bakery nestled in a quiet alleyway off the Damascus Gate in the Old City of Jerusalem, and it holds a revered status as a must-stop destination for locals and visitors alike seeking an evening warm snack fix, particularly their renowned egg pies. Operating primarily during the night hours, Abu Ali tirelessly supplies the city with ka'ak and bread, while also skilfully making these steaming pies for passers-by.

The dough here is similar to the pan-fried turmeric bread (page 241), with the edges deftly pinched to create an open pie ready to be filled with an array of savory toppings before baking. Preparation is key here. Have all your ingredients chopped and prepped beforehand, as once you begin rolling and assembling, speed is essential. Depending on your oven size, you may need to bake the pies in batches, but the effort will undoubtedly yield warm, satisfying pies that pay homage to Abu Ali's legacy, as well as being utterly irresistible.

Egg, onion & feta open pie

Aqras Beyd

For the dough
1 tsp fast-acting (instant) dried yeast
1½ tsp granulated sugar
¾ cup plus 2 tbsp | 200ml lukewarm water
3 cups | 13¼ oz | 375g all-purpose flour, plus more for dusting
2½ tbsp milk powder (optional)
1 tbsp olive oil, plus more for greasing

To make the dough, put the yeast, sugar and 7 tbsp | 100ml of the water into a small bowl. Mix well and set aside for about 5 minutes, or until the mixture starts to bubble.

Place the flour, milk powder and 1 teaspoon of salt in the bowl of a stand mixer with the dough hook attachment in place. Mix on low speed for just 1 minute, for the ingredients to combine. Increase the speed to medium, then slowly pour in the yeast mixture, followed by the oil—it will start to form a shaggy mass at first. Slowly add the remaining 7 tbsp | 100ml of water, then keep the machine running for 7–8 minutes, until the dough comes together as a ball. If the dough seems dry, add more water, 1 tablespoon at a time, until soft and smooth. You want it to be smooth and elastic and for the dough not to stick to your fingers when pinched.

Transfer the dough to a lightly oiled bowl, then cover with a clean kitchen towel and leave somewhere warm for about 1 hour, until the dough has risen by a third.

Transfer the dough to a lightly floured work surface, then cut it into 4 pieces and shape each piece into a round ball. Cover with a slightly damp kitchen towel and leave to rest for 10 minutes—you won't see any change in size or shape after 10 minutes but it's still important for the dough to have this "rest."

After 10 minutes, flatten each ball of dough one at a time, first with your fingers and then using a rolling pin to shape them into

recipe continues

For the filling

3 tbsp olive oil

3 onions, peeled, halved and finely sliced (3½ cups | 450g)

2 medium zucchini (11¼ oz | 320g), halved lengthwise, seeds scooped out, and cut lengthwise into 8 batons

4 eggs

salt and black pepper

4 green onions, finely sliced (2 oz | 55g)

3½ oz | 100g feta cheese, crumbled into roughly 1-inch | 2½cm chunks (¾ cup)

¼ cup | 5g fresh oregano leaves

1 tbsp za'atar (optional)

For the adha

3 tbsp olive oil

2 tsp Aleppo chile flakes (or regular chile flakes)

9-inch | 23cm wide circles; use more flour to dust the work surface if you need to, to prevent them sticking as you roll. Take care not to have any tears in the dough. Continue until all the balls of dough are rolled out, covering them with a damp kitchen towel once rolled, to prevent them drying out. Set aside to proof for a final 20 minutes.

While the dough is proofing, adjust the racks to the upper- and lower-middle positions and preheat the oven to 475°F. Place two baking sheets in the oven to heat up.

To make the filling, put 2 tablespoons of the oil into a medium sauté pan and place over medium heat. Cook the onions for about 15 minutes, or until golden and caramelized. Remove from the heat, transfer the onions to a small bowl and set aside until needed. Add the rest of the oil to the same pan and gently fry the zucchini for about 6–8 minutes, until slightly softened but still holding their shape.

To make the adha, put the olive oil and chile flakes into a small saucepan and warm through for a minute, to combine. Remove from the heat and set aside.

When ready to bake, working quickly, remove the hot baking sheets from the oven, line with parchment paper and place 2 rounds of dough on each baking sheet. Bake for 2 minutes, until they slightly puff up. You don't want them to take any color at this stage. Remove from the oven, let cool slightly and carefully start pinching the edges of the bread to form a flan-like lip that is about ¼-inch | ½cm high.

Spread a quarter of the caramelized onions over the base of each round and break an egg on top. Use a fork to swirl it around, making sure the egg reaches all over the onions, and season well with salt and a good grind of black pepper. Divide the zucchini, green onion and feta between the pies, followed by a few oregano leaves and the za'atar (if using).

Return to the oven and bake for 10–14 minutes, switching and rotating the baking sheets halfway through cooking, until the egg is cooked through and the base is golden-brown. If the egg still needs some help cooking, place it under a hot broiler for 1–2 minutes.

Serve warm or at room temperature, spooning the adha over just before serving.

This is a great way to share bread with family and friends as part of a meal, or as a light supper with a cup of tea. The bread can be shaped all sorts of ways: into a flatbread, a loaf or individual buns, as here. Either way, it should always be super soft—almost moist—in the middle, with a really golden crust.

Cheese & sumac bites

Aqras Jeben

For the dough
1½ tsp fast-acting (instant) yeast
1½ tsp granulated sugar
¾ cup | 170ml lukewarm water
2½ cups | 11¼ oz | 320g
   all-purpose flour
salt
6 tbsp | 90ml sunflower oil,
   plus more for greasing
1 medium egg
1 tbsp milk
1 tbsp nigella seeds

For the filling
7 oz | 200g feta cheese,
   crumbled (1½ cups)
½ cup | 10g fresh parsley,
   finely chopped
3 green onions, finely sliced
   (3 oz | 80g)
2 tbsp sumac
½ tsp Aleppo chile flakes
   (or regular chile flakes)
3 tbsp olive oil

Put the yeast, sugar and water into a small bowl and whisk to combine. Set aside for 5 minutes, until it starts to bubble.

Put the flour and 1¼ teaspoons of salt into the bowl of a stand mixer with the dough hook in place. Mix for 1 minute, just to combine, then add the yeast mixture, followed by the sunflower oil. Work on low speed for about 1 minute, to bring everything together, then increase the speed to medium. Continue to mix for 5 minutes, until the dough is soft and elastic.

Form the dough into a ball, then grease the bowl with 1 teaspoon of oil and put the dough inside. Turn it a couple of times so that it's completely coated in oil, then cover the bowl with a clean kitchen towel. Set aside somewhere warm for 1–1½ hours, until it has doubled in size.

Put all the ingredients for the filling into a medium bowl, mix well and set aside.

Divide the dough into 20 even pieces, about 1 oz | 25g each. Roll each piece into a ball, place them on a large plate, cover with a clean kitchen towel and set aside to rest for 10 minutes.

Preheat the oven to 425°F. Line a 12-inch | 30cm round cake pan or 9 x 13-inch | 23 x 33cm baking pan (any shape will work) with parchment paper.

On a clean work surface, use your fingers to flatten each ball into a round disc, about 4 inches | 10cm wide. Spoon 1 tablespoon (about ⅓ oz | 10g) of the cheese mixture into the center of each disc, then draw the sides upwards and press together to form a ball.

Arrange the buns in the prepared pan, slightly spaced apart. In a small bowl, whisk the egg with the milk and egg-wash the buns all over, then sprinkle with the nigella seeds. Set aside to rest for 5 minutes, then bake for about 20 minutes, rotating the pan halfway through, until the buns are cooked and the bottoms are golden brown. Remove from the oven and serve warm or at room temperature.

The dough can be made up to 1 day ahead and kept in the fridge, ready to be rolled and baked. Once baked the buns also freeze well, ready to be warmed through in the oven straight from frozen.

sweets

Palestinians eat sweets throughout the day, not just as dessert at the end of a meal. Their obsession with sweet things goes back hundreds of years. From a simple vermicelli cooked with sugar, butter and a sprinkle of cinnamon, to a more decadent-rich phyllo drenched in floral sugar syrup, to elaborate delicate cookies flavored with rose water, orange blossom, cardamom and Arabic mastic. As with many of the dishes in the Palestinian repertoire, we are not shy of using bold flavors that are steeped in layers of the history of the region.

Some of my fondest childhood memories involve fair amounts of baklava, knafeh, assortments of cookies and biscuits, which inspire the recipes in this chapter.

Apricot orchards have survived in many Palestinian towns and villages such as Beit Jala, Jifna, Salfit, Sebastia and Balaa, but in other areas they have become a distant memory for many Palestinians. Even the wild apricot, called al-hasum, previously widespread in the forest of Safed, became extinct. Other Palestinian apricot varieties are Mestikawi, Wardi, Lauzi and Kalabi.

This is a classic combination of apricot and almond that works together perfectly. I have added lemon zest and orange blossom water for an extra fragrant cake.

Apricot, orange & almond cake

Ka'ket Mishmash w Burtuqal

¾ cup | 5¼ oz | 150g soft dried apricots
2 large oranges, one zested and both juiced (to give 7 tbsp | 100ml orange juice)
2 tbsp orange blossom water
10 tbsp | 150g unsalted butter, at room temperature, plus more for greasing
½ cup plus 3 tbsp | 5 oz | 135g granulated sugar
salt
zest of 1 lemon
½ cup | 150g Greek yogurt
1½ tsp ground cinnamon
3 large eggs, lightly whisked
2 cups | 6⅓ oz | 180g almond flour
½ cup plus 3 tbsp | 3½ oz | 100g polenta (I use instant polenta)
1 tsp baking powder
1 tsp vanilla bean paste
5–6 fresh apricots, cut in half lengthwise (9½ oz | 270g)

For the almond clusters
1 egg white
¾ cup | 25g sliced almonds
1 tbsp confectioners' sugar, plus more for dusting

For the glaze
¼ cup apricot jam
2 tbsp water

Preheat the oven to 350°F. Lightly grease a 9-inch | 23cm springform cake pan and line the base with parchment paper.

Roughly chop the dried apricots and put them into a small bowl. Add the orange zest and juice and orange blossom water and set aside.

Put the butter and sugar into the bowl of a stand mixer with a paddle attachment in place, and mix on medium speed for 2–3 minutes, until thick and smooth. Add ½ teaspoon of salt and the remaining cake ingredients, apart from the fresh apricot halves, beat well for 2 minutes, then fold in the dried apricots and orange juice.

Pour the mixture into the prepared pan and spread out evenly. Cover and let it rest for 10 minutes, then arrange the apricot halves on top, cut side up, making sure not to press them hard into the batter. Bake for 30–40 minutes, or until the surface is lightly browned and the cake pulls away slightly from the sides of the pan, then cover loosely with foil to prevent the top browning too much and bake for 20–30 minutes more, or until a skewer inserted in the center comes out clean. Remove the foil and allow the cake to cool completely in the pan.

While the cake is cooling, put all the ingredients for the almond clusters into a small bowl and mix well. Spread about 1 teaspoon portions of the mixture on a lightly oiled parchment-lined baking sheet, spreading each out so that the nuts are slightly overlapping (you should have about 15 pieces), and bake for 12 minutes, until lightly browned. Remove from the oven and allow to cool down completely.

Finally, to make the glaze, whisk the jam with the water in a small bowl, then brush it on top of the cake. Finish with the almond clusters and dust with confectioners' sugar before serving.

This cake will keep for 5 days in a cool place.

This is a version of the Greek milopita cake, traditionally made with olive oil and yogurt. It can be served as a dessert with a dollop of your choice of whipped cream, or with a cup of coffee for breakfast. Pear or quince can replace the apple in this cake for an equally delicious result.

This same cake has been made among the Palestinian Greek Orthodox community in Bethlehem and Beit Jala, south Jerusalem, according to eighty-nine-year-old Mary Anastas—my doctor's mother-in-law, who grew up in the area and has raised ten children. Mary is a great cook who learned her cooking skills from her late mother-in-law. In later years, Mary has been devoting her time to writing and has published a number of books about Palestinian culture.

Spiced apple, walnut & lemon cake

Ka'ket Tuffah w Jawz

1¼ cups | 300ml sunflower oil, plus more for greasing
1½ cups plus 2 tbsp | 11¼ oz | 320g granulated sugar
1 tsp vanilla bean paste
3 large eggs
4 Granny Smith apples, peeled, cored and cut into ¾-inch | 2cm cubes (1 lb | 460g)
2 tbsp lemon juice
3⅔ cups | 16 oz | 450g all-purpose flour, plus more for dusting
1½ tsp ground cinnamon
¾ tsp ground allspice
⅛ tsp ground cloves
1 tsp baking soda
salt
1¼ cups | 150g walnuts, finely chopped

For the glaze
1¼ cups | 5⅔ oz | 160g confectioners' sugar
2 tbsp lemon juice

Preheat the oven to 350°F.

Grease a 12-cup | 24cm bundt (fluted cake pan) and dust it well with about 2 tablespoons of flour, making sure the flour is well distributed. Tip the pan over your kitchen sink to get rid of any excess flour and set aside.

Put the sunflower oil, sugar and vanilla into the bowl of a stand mixer, with a paddle attachment in place, and mix on high speed for 3 minutes, until the mixture is pale and smooth. While the mixer is running, add the eggs, one a time.

Put the apples and the lemon juice into a large bowl, mix well and set aside.

Sift all the dry ingredients, using a fine sieve, and add them to the egg mixture, along with 1 teaspoon of salt, the apples and walnuts. Mix for a minute or so on low speed, until well combined—you don't want to overwork it—then tip the batter into the prepared pan. Even it out with a spatula and bake for 70–80 minutes, or until a skewer inserted in the center comes out clean.

Allow the cake to cool down completely before removing it from the pan. When the cake has cooled, put the confectioners' sugar and lemon juice into a medium bowl and whisk well, until the mixture is very smooth. If the mixture is too thick, add a few more drops of lemon juice or cold water.

Place the cake on a serving plate and drizzle the glaze all over it. Set aside for a few minutes, to allow the glaze to set slightly.

This cake freezes well, and I freeze leftovers by wrapping them in parchment paper and popping them into a sealable bag.

Imagine yourself sitting in one of many coffee shops dotted around the souk in Jerusalem's old city, having a piece of chocolate and a strong, sweet Arabic cardamom coffee. One mouthful of this dessert can almost definitely transport you there. It's a dessert meant for sharing, to be spooned straight from the pan. A great, easy, chewy and fudgy brownie which can be ready in under 20 minutes. It hits all the right spots for chocolate lovers like me.

Pan-baked tahini, halva & coffee brownie

Qahwa w Halaweh Brownie

Rounded ½ cup | 150g tahini paste
½ cup | 120ml lukewarm water
Heaping ½ cup | 3¾ oz | 110g granulated sugar
2 large eggs
¼ cup | 20g unsweetened cocoa powder
1 tbsp instant espresso coffee
¼ cup | 1 oz | 30g all-purpose flour
½ tsp ground cardamom
⅛ tsp ground cloves
½ tsp baking powder
salt
1½ oz | 40g dark chocolate chips or chocolate roughly chopped into ¼-inch | ½cm pieces (70% cocoa solids) (⅓ cup chopped)

For the toppings
1½ tbsp sesame seeds
1½ oz | 40g dark chocolate chips or chocolate roughly chopped into ¼-inch | ½cm pieces (70% cocoa solids) (⅓ cup chopped)
⅓ cup | 70g plain or vanilla halva, broken into chunks
vanilla ice cream

Preheat the oven to 375°F. Grease a 8-inch | 22cm square baking pan or dish with sunflower oil and set aside.

Put the tahini and water into the bowl of a stand mixer, with the paddle attachment in place, and mix on medium-high speed for 2 minutes, until pale and smooth. Reduce to low speed, add the sugar, then the eggs, one at a time, and mix for a further 2 minutes.

Sift all the dry ingredients, using a fine sieve, and add them to the tahini mixture, along with a heaping ¼ teaspoon of salt and the chocolate. Mix for a minute more. Pour the batter into the prepared pan.

Sprinkle the top with the sesame seeds and chocolate and dot with the halva. Bake for 10–12 minutes, until the edges are set and the center is not runny (it needs to be slightly wet). Set aside for 10 minutes before serving.

Serve with vanilla ice cream.

The brownie can be stored in the fridge for up to a week.

This is my contemporary twist on a Palestinian ma'amoul. What is better than ma'amoul cookies? Ma'amoul chocolate bars, of course! Made with the traditional ma'amoul filling ingredients of rich dates and nuts, and flavored with hints of rose water, cardamom and anise, the bars are then drizzled with dark chocolate.

   These bars are guaranteed to be popular, with everyone coming back for seconds and thirds. Little do they know they are vegan.

Chocolate date bars

Ma'amoul bil Shukulata

2½ cups | 250g walnuts
¼ cup | 60g date paste (or 2¼ oz | 60g pitted medjool dates, finely chopped, plus 1 tbsp sunflower oil)
5 oz | 140g vegan chocolate digestive biscuits, broken into fine crumbs (about 9 biscuits)
packed ½ cup | 100g dark muscovado sugar
¾ tsp ground cardamom
1 tsp ground cinnamon
¾ tsp ground anise seed
½ tsp mahlab
salt
2 tbsp runny honey or agave syrup
2 tbsp rose water
7 oz | 200g vegan dark chocolate (70% cocoa solids), broken into roughly ½-inch | 1cm pieces
¼ oz | 5g freeze-dried raspberries
2 tbsp pistachios, finely crushed

Preheat the oven to 375°F. Line a 9 x 13-inch | 23 x 33cm baking dish with parchment paper.

Place the walnuts in the prepared dish and toast for 8–10 minutes. Remove from the oven and set aside to cool completely. Once cool, place in the bowl of a food processor and chop finely—be sure not to overprocess.

If using dates rather than the paste, put the dates and sunflower oil into a small pan and place over low heat. Cook for 5 minutes, stirring frequently, to form a mushy, sticky paste. Remove from the heat and set aside.

Place the chopped walnuts, biscuit crumbs, sugar, spices and ½ teaspoon of salt in a medium bowl and mix well to combine, then add the date paste, honey and rose water, and knead thoroughly. Use your hands to make sure the mixture becomes fully incorporated.

Spread the mixture onto the now empty 9 x 13-inch | 25 x 30cm baking sheet, and press it down firmly. Place the baking dish in the fridge for at least 2 hours, or overnight.

In a double boiler or in a medium heatproof bowl set over a pot of gently simmering water, melt the chocolate until smooth and shiny. Drizzle the melted chocolate in a thin stream over the cookie base and sprinkle with the dried raspberries and crushed pistachios. Leave for 1 hour to firm up before cutting into squares.

Dates are an essential ingredient in Palestinian baking and sweets—to name a few, ma'amoul, ka'ak and mabrouseh. Dates have always been used as a natural and healthy way to add sweetness, and they give a contrast in texture and flavor, infused with aromatic spices.

These cookies are based on a draft recipe my sister Kawthar handed me a while ago when I asked her to show me how she makes them. We all gathered at Eid Al Fitr at her house in the Beit Hanina neighborhood, in East Jerusalem. Kawthar is the best cook in the family, and she can effortlessly rustle up a lunch or dinner party in no time. She is the one who's always eager and willing to roll up her sleeves and give a hand to other members of the family, by cooking or making sweets and cookies for any celebration.

Date & nigella seed rolls

Makrouta

¾ cup | 3½ oz | 100g all-purpose flour, plus a little more for dusting
⅓ cup | 1¾ oz | 50g fine semolina
heaping ¼ tsp baking powder
⅛ tsp baking soda
1½ tbsp confectioners' sugar
½ tsp ground anise seeds
heaping ¼ tsp ground fennel seeds
salt
4 tsp sesame seeds
1½ tsp nigella seeds
zest of ½ a lemon
½ tsp vanilla bean paste
4 tbsp | 60g butter, melted
1 tbsp sunflower oil
2 tbsp | 30ml lukewarm water
confectioners' sugar, for dusting (optional)

For the date filling
¾ cup | 7 oz | 200g date paste
1 tbsp unsalted butter, at room temperature
½ tbsp sunflower oil

Put the flour, semolina, baking powder, baking soda, confectioners' sugar, spices and ⅛ teaspoon of salt into a fine sieve over a medium bowl and sift everything—this also helps to mix all the dry ingredients together.

Add the sesame seeds, nigella seeds, lemon zest, vanilla, melted butter and sunflower oil, and mix well. Using your hand, slowly add the water while kneading for 1–2 minutes until you have a smooth, elastic dough that does not stick. Cover with a clean kitchen towel and leave to rest in the fridge for 20 minutes.

Meanwhile, combine the date paste, butter and sunflower oil in a small bowl, and knead together to form a smooth filling.

Preheat the oven to 400°F.

Divide the dough in half. Dust the work surface with a little flour and roll the dough into a rectangle, roughly 6 x 10 inches | 15 x 25cm. Cut it lengthwise into three strips, each 2 x 10 inches | 5 x 25cm.

Take ⅙ of the date paste and roll it into a thin sausage 10 inches | 25cm long, making sure it's the same thickness the whole way along. Lay the date paste along the edge of one of the strips of dough, and carefully roll it twice over, until all the date paste is covered—use a bench scraper to gently ease the dough away from the work surface. Don't worry too much about little tears—these can be patched up quite easily, as the dough is easy to work with.

recipe continues

Turn the pieces over so that the "joint" is facing down, and cut diagonally into diamond-shaped rolls about 1½ inches / 4cm long. Repeat with the rest of the dough and date paste—you should end up with about 35 rolls.

Arrange the rolls on a parchment-lined baking sheet, then, using the tines of a fork, make a couple of little indentations in the top of each roll.

Bake for 10–12 minutes, until slightly golden. Remove from the oven and allow to cool down.

Optional: Dust with confectioners' sugar immediately before serving.

Many countries across the world today share and enjoy a form of these sweet or savory double-baked cakes or bread. In Palestine we call both types arshaleh—arshaleh helweh and arshaleh malhaa. They are great dunking cookies to have with a cup of tea or coffee, or to soak in sweetened warm milk for breakfast.

Arshaleh are relatively easy to make and great to gift for Christmas, Eid or any celebration.

Anise & sesame rusks

Arshaleh

2 cups plus 3 tbsp | 9½ oz | 270g all-purpose flour
1 cup plus 2 tbsp | 8 oz | 220g granulated sugar
2 tbsp finely ground anise seed
2 tsp anise seeds
1 tsp baking powder
heaping ¼ tsp baking soda
3 large eggs
1 tsp vanilla bean paste
7 tbsp | 100ml olive oil
7 tbsp | 100ml sunflower oil

For the garnish
2 tbsp white sesame seeds

Preheat the oven to 375°F. Grease the base and sides of a 9 x 13-inch | 25 x 30cm baking dish and line with parchment paper, then set aside.

Place the dry ingredients in a medium bowl and mix well to combine, then set aside.

Put the eggs and vanilla into the bowl of a stand mixer, with the paddle attachment in place, and mix on high speed for 2 minutes, until the mixture is pale. Reduce the speed to medium and add the oils, then add the dry ingredients and mix for 2 minutes just until combined—you don't want to overwork it.

Tip the mixture into the prepared dish and even out with a spatula. Sprinkle the top with the sesame seeds and bake on the middle rack of the oven for 30 minutes, until the sides and the top have taken some color.

Remove from the oven and set aside to cool down completely, then cut the cake in half lengthwise using a serrated knife and slice each half into 15 slices, each about ¾ x 4½ inches | 2 x 11cm. Arrange the slices on a parchment-lined baking sheet and bake at the same temperature for 20 minutes on each side, turning the slices in between, until golden brown.

Let the rusks cool completely before storing them in an airtight container. They keep for a few weeks in a cool place.

Middle Eastern ma'akaroon have nothing to do with French macarons. The Middle Eastern ones are traditionally made from semolina, olive oil and aniseed and are deep-fried before being drenched in sugar syrup.

Here is a slightly healthier way of making these buttery cookies, which are pretty easy to make. I like to make a big batch of these and gift them at Christmas.

Lemon & pistachio cookies

Ma'akaroon

1 cup | 125g pistachios, finely ground
1¼ cups | 125g almond flour
½ cup | 100g granulated sugar
½ tsp mastic, ground
heaping ¼ tsp baking powder
salt
2 tsp finely chopped preserved lemon
1 tsp lemon zest
1 tsp vanilla bean paste
1 tbsp runny honey
1 egg, lightly whisked
1 tbsp unsalted butter, at room temperature
2–3 tbsp confectioners' sugar, sifted

Put the ground pistachios, almond flour, granulated sugar, mastic, baking powder and ⅛ teaspoon of salt into a large bowl and mix well, just enough to combine everything together. Add the preserved lemon, lemon zest, vanilla, honey, egg and butter and give everything a good stir, using a wooden spoon or spatula. The mixture should be slightly sticky.

Place the confectioners' sugar on a large plate and start rolling the batter into walnut-size balls, about 1 oz | 30g each. Gently roll the balls in the confectioners' sugar, making sure that they are well coated on all sides. Arrange on a large baking sheet lined with parchment paper, evenly spaced out. Cover the baking sheet and leave in the fridge for 30 minutes.

Preheat the oven to 375°F and bake the cookies for 10–12 minutes, or until they start to get a bit of color. Leave them to cool completely before serving.

Once the cookies have been rolled, they can be kept in the freezer, in an airtight container, for a few weeks. When they are already baked, they will keep in an airtight container for 5 days.

Antebikh or ainabia is a typical Hebron cooked grape preserve, made with the grape's seeds and anise seeds, which gives it a distinctive taste.

Rice pudding is a popular dish in the Arab world and often gets treated as a dish to snack on, rather than a dessert, as it's filling, comforting and inexpensive to make. Adding tahini to a sweet rice pudding is not typical in the renowned dessert, but it works perfectly in this recipe, making it soft and creamy. The pudding is light and fragrant with the flavors of anise seed and rose water.

Tahini rice pudding with grape compote

Helou al Ruz ma' Antebikh

For the pudding
¾ cup plus 2 tbsp | 175g Egyptian, risotto or other short-grain rice
1 quart | 1 liter water
salt
heaping ¼ tsp ground turmeric
packed ⅓ cup | 80g light brown sugar
⅓ cup | 90g tahini paste
2 tsp rose water

For the grape compote
1 lb 2 oz | 500g black or red seedless grapes
heaping ¼ tsp ground anise seeds
2 tbsp olive oil

For the garnish
1 tbsp butter
2 tbsp toasted pine nuts

Rinse the rice and soak in plenty of cold water for 1 hour.

While the rice is soaking, make the grape compote: place all the ingredients in a medium saucepan and bring to a boil, then cook over medium-low heat, until the grapes are starting to soften and collapse—about 15 minutes. Lightly crush some of the grapes with the back of a spoon and set aside to cool down.

In the meantime, place the butter and pine nuts in a small pan and cook over medium heat, stirring the whole time for 3–4 minutes, or until the pine nuts are golden brown. Transfer the nuts to a plate lined with paper towels and set aside.

Put the drained rice into a large saucepan, along with 2½ cups | 600ml of the water, a heaping ¼ teaspoon of salt and the turmeric. Bring to a boil, then cook over medium-high heat, stirring frequently, for 7 minutes. Decrease the heat and add the sugar, tahini, rose water and the remaining 1½ cups | 400ml of water, and cook for about 7 minutes until thickened—the rice should still retain a bite.

Remove from the heat and pour the rice into individual serving bowls. Allow to cool slightly before serving, or cover and chill for a couple of hours.

When ready to serve, spoon some of the grape compote on top of each pudding and garnish with the toasted pine nuts.

Some of my favorite seasonal mangoes are Alphonso, Ataúlfo and Kent. This is a clever and yet easy way of preparing a refreshing dessert that is perfect as a summer treat. In winter frozen mangoes are handy for making this impressive, layered dessert.

The parfait can also be made in a large glass bowl, for individual portions to be served at the table. Whichever way you choose, this parfait will for sure impress your guests.

Mango & salted seeds parfait

Helou al Manga

2 large or 4 small very ripe
  mangoes
2 tbsp | 25g granulated sugar
zest and juice of 2 limes
1¾ cups | 450ml heavy cream
1 tsp vanilla bean paste

For the crumble
½ cup | 60g panko breadcrumbs
6 tbsp | 60g sunflower seeds,
  roughly chopped
4 tbsp | 50g unsalted butter,
  melted
1 tsp vanilla bean paste
½ tsp ground cinnamon
salt

Preheat the oven to 375°F. Line a baking dish with parchment paper.

To make the crumble, place the breadcrumbs and seeds in the prepared baking dish and roast for 10 minutes, until golden. Remove from the oven and set aside to cool.

Put all the ingredients for the crumble, including the crumbs and seeds, into a medium bowl with ¼ teaspoon of salt and mix well. Set aside.

Peel and pit the mangoes—you should end up with about 1 lb 5 oz | 600g of mango flesh. Place 14 oz | 400g of the flesh into a freestanding blender, along with half the sugar and half the lime juice and zest, and blend for 1 minute or until it forms a smooth purée.

Finely chop the remaining mango flesh and put it into a small bowl. Add the rest of the lime juice and zest and mix well. Cover and keep chilled.

Put the cream, remaining sugar and vanilla into the bowl of a stand mixer, with a whisk attachment in place, and whisk on a high speed for 1–2 minutes, until stiff peaks form. Set a quarter of the cream aside. Add the mango purée to the rest of the cream and fold until well incorporated, then set aside.

Put about 2 tablespoons of the crumble mixture in the bottom of six serving glasses or bowls, then top with the mango cream and leave to chill for at least a couple of hours.

When ready to serve, top each glass with the mango salsa and the whipped cream, and finally sprinkle the rest of the crumble on top.

Sweets

Karawiyah is a delightful dessert with a delicate texture and a fragrant flavor. It's a simple vegan treat that's often made after a childbirth.

Karawiyah is like many dishes in the Palestinian repertoire, essentially using the ingredients that are available to create tasty treats. The pudding can be served warm or at room temperature, but I prefer to eat it chilled.

Caraway & nut pudding

Karawiyah

1 quart | 1 liter dairy-free milk
  or water
1½ oz | 45g cornstarch
1 tsp vanilla bean paste
1 tbsp ground caraway seeds
2 tsp ground anise seeds
heaping ¼ tsp ground cinnamon,
  plus more for sprinkling
⅛ tsp ground cloves
7 tbsp | 100ml agave syrup

For the topping
¼ cup | 40g walnuts, toasted
  (see page 35 for how best to
  do this) and lightly crushed
¼ cup | 25g sliced almonds,
  toasted
3 tbsp | 30g pistachios,
  toasted and roughly chopped
¼ cup | 40g golden or
  regular raisins

In a medium saucepan, whisk together the milk or water, cornstarch, vanilla and ground spices until the cornstarch has dissolved. Cook over medium heat for 5 minutes, whisking from time to time until it starts to release steam, then whisk in the agave syrup and keep whisking for 4 minutes, until the mixture has thickened to a custard-like consistency.

Remove from the heat and pour into a shallow baking dish or serving dish. Cover with plastic wrap, making sure the plastic wrap touches the surface (this is to prevent the pudding forming a skin). Allow to cool, and serve at room temperature, or chilled, with the nuts and dried fruit scattered over and a sprinkle of cinnamon.

I have often made roast plums and other stone fruit over the years. It's a simple dessert, yet nothing beats the scent of warm, spice-spiked fruit filling the space around the table after dinner. Double the number of plums and have some of the leftovers for breakfast with yogurt, or on warm toast spread with labneh or cream cheese.

Sumac roast plums with cardamom cream & pistachio

Barquq bil Sumac w al Creama

8 plums (13 oz | 366g)
3 cardamom pods
1 tsp sumac
3 tbsp runny honey
zest of ½ orange
1 tsp lemon juice
1 tbsp water
1¼ cups | 300ml heavy cream
3 tsp honey
heaping ¼ tsp ground cardamom

For the candied pistachios
¼ cup | 45g granulated sugar
heaping ¼ tsp ground cinnamon
3 tbsp water
salt
7 tbsp | 70g pistachios

Preheat the oven to 400°F.

Halve and pit the plums, then place cut side up in a roasting pan or baking dish in which they can lie snugly in a single layer.

Crack the cardamom pods, then tip the seeds into a mortar and pestle and grind them to a fine powder. Mix with the sumac, honey, orange zest, lemon juice and water, then drizzle this mixture over the fruit. Bake for about 20 minutes, or until the plums are almost collapsing.

Meanwhile, make the candied pistachios. Line a baking sheet with parchment paper, and have it ready next to the stove. Put the sugar, cinnamon, water and ⅛ teaspoon of salt into a large sauté pan over medium heat. Cook until the sugar has almost dissolved, stirring occasionally. Add the pistachios and continue to cook for 3–4 minutes, stirring occasionally (to avoid the nuts browning too much), until all the liquid has evaporated and you can see crystallization forming on the nuts. Tip the nuts onto the lined baking sheet, and quickly spread them out to separate them. Leave to cool completely.

Place the cream, honey and ground cardamom in the bowl of a stand mixer, with a whisk attachment in place, and whip the cream on a medium speed for about 3 minutes, or until soft peaks form.

When ready to serve, divide the fruit and whipped cream between four plates and add a generous scattering of the candied pistachios.

The only two competitive ice cream makers in Palestine, Al Arz and Rukab, are both family-run businesses. They started around 1940 as a homemade ice cream affair, which would then be sold by vendors in the streets of Jerusalem, Ramallah and other major cities around Palestine. Both companies are still running and have a great turnover.

Palestinian ice cream, often referred to as bouza or Arabic ice cream, is a delicious and unique frozen treat with a distinctive texture and flavor. It's known for being stretchy and chewy, thanks to the use of ingredients like mastic (a resin) and salep, also known as sahlab (a starchy orchid root extract).

Some popular flavors of Palestinian ice cream include pistachio, rose water and various fruit. It's often garnished with chopped nuts or served in a sesame-crusted cone. Palestinian ice cream is a beloved dessert in the Middle East and can be found in ice cream shops and street stalls throughout the region.

Labneh & pomegranate ice cream

Bouza bil Labneh w al Rumman

seeds from 1–2 pomegranates (10½ oz | 300g), plus more for garnish
7 tbsp | 120g labneh (page 23)
14 oz | 385g condensed milk
zest and juice of 2 limes (¼ cup | 60ml juice)
2 tbsp rose water
salt
1¼ cups | 300ml heavy cream
2 tbsp confectioners' sugar
extra-virgin olive oil, for drizzling

Place the pomegranate seeds in a stand blender and blend on high speed for 2 minutes, until they form a smooth paste. Pour the mixture into a fine sieve placed over a bowl and drain all the juice, using the back of a spoon to help push it into the bowl. You'll need ¾ cup plus 2 tbsp | 200ml of juice in total.

Put the pomegranate juice, labneh, condensed milk, lime zest and juice, rose water and a heaping ¼ teaspoon of salt into a large bowl and mix well until smooth. Set aside.

Put the cream and confectioners' sugar into the bowl of a stand mixer, with a whisk attachment in place, and whisk on high speed for 2–3 minutes, until it is airy and stiff peaks form. Add about a quarter of the whipped cream to the pomegranate and labneh mixture and gently mix it in with a rubber spatula, until well incorporated.

Add the rest of the whipped cream and fold it in, running the spatula down the sides and along the bottom of bowl, then lifting it up through the center, taking care not to overmix.

Spoon the mixture into a 5 x 9-inch | 2-liter loaf pan or airtight container roughly that size. Cover with plastic wrap or an airtight silicone lid and freeze until solid, at least 6 hours.

To serve, transfer the ice cream to the fridge and let it soften for 10 minutes before scooping into bowls. Garnish with a good sprinkle of pomegranate seeds and a drizzle of extra-virgin olive oil.

These gorgeous coconut truffles are made with sweetened condensed milk and dipped in chocolate. A heavenly treat that is perfect for sharing; they are easy to make and ready in no time.

Coconut, rose & chocolate truffles

Jawz al Hind bil Shukulata

2¾ cups | 240g fine desiccated coconut
¾ cup | 180ml vegan (or dairy) condensed milk
1 tsp coconut oil
1 tsp vanilla bean paste
salt
9 oz | 260g dark cooking chocolate (75% cocoa solids), roughly chopped

For the garnish
flaked sea salt
dried rose petals
ground pistachios (optional)

In a large bowl, mix together the desiccated coconut, condensed milk, coconut oil, vanilla and ½ teaspoon of salt until well combined.

Place the mixture in the fridge for about 30 minutes, to firm up.

Once the mixture is firm enough to handle, take small portions and roll them into truffle-size balls (about ½ oz | 15g each).

Place the rolled truffles on a baking sheet lined with parchment paper and put them back into the fridge for an additional 20 minutes.

While the truffles are chilling, melt the dark chocolate in the microwave, using a double boiler or in a medium heatproof bowl set over a pot of gently simmering water.

Once the truffles have firmed up, dip each one into the melted dark chocolate, making sure to coat them completely.

Return the coated truffles to the parchment-lined baking sheet, sprinkle on a little flaked sea salt, dried rose petals and ground pistachios (if using), and let them set in the fridge for at least 15–20 minutes, or until the chocolate hardens.

The star of the show here is of course knafeh (see glossary, page 308), a national institution in Palestine and as popular in neighboring countries. The crème de la crème of knafeh comes from Nablus, where this exquisite dessert was allegedly first invented and made.

I'd like to tell you a little bit about ashtah. Ashtah is the Middle Eastern equivalent of clotted cream. Many Palestinian and Middle Eastern desserts use ashtah, which varies from one country to another. In Lebanon, ashtah is made in the same way as clotted cream—milk is simmered and the sticky film that forms on the top is collected. It's a slow and time-consuming process. Other ways of making ashtah include adding vinegar or lemon to boiling milk to stimulate the curdling for collection from the top of the milk. In this recipe, I have sped the process up by making a combination of milk and cream that is thickened with cornstarch.

To get ahead with preparations for the pie, the ashtah and the sugar syrup can be made 1–2 days in advance.

Ashtah knafeh pie

Knafeh bil Ashtah

2 cups | 500ml whole milk

1 cup | 250ml heavy cream

2 tbsp granulated sugar

⅓ cup | 45g cornstarch

½ tsp mastic

1 tbsp orange blossom water

14 oz | 400g fresh or frozen
knafeh (kataifi) pastry
(available in most Middle
Eastern and Turkish shops),
thawed if frozen

¾ cup plus 2 tbsp | 200g
unsalted butter, melted

½ cup | 70g pistachios,
finely chopped

For the sugar syrup

1½ cups | 300g granulated sugar

¾ cup plus 2 tbsp | 200ml water

2 tablespoons lemon juice

1½ tablespoons orange blossom
water

First, make the syrup. Put the sugar into a small saucepan with the water and place over medium-high heat. Bring to a boil and add the lemon juice. Cook for 5 minutes, stirring a few times with a wooden spoon. Stir in the orange blossom water and take the syrup off the heat. Set aside and allow the syrup to cool completely.

Place the milk, cream, 1 tablespoon of the sugar and the cornstarch in a medium saucepan and whisk well until the cornstarch has dissolved.

Place the remaining 1 tablespoon of sugar and the mastic in a mortar and pestle, and grind until smooth. Whisk this into the milk and cream mixture, then place over medium heat and bring to a gentle boil, whisking the whole time for about 5 minutes or until it's thickened and has the consistency of thick custard.

Whisk in the orange blossom water and remove from the heat. Pour the ashtah into a deep bowl or baking dish and cover the surface with plastic wrap, making sure that the plastic wrap touches the top of the ashtah, to prevent it forming a skin. Set aside to cool down for 30 minutes, and store in the fridge until needed (ashtah should be cold before it can be used).

Preheat the oven to 400°F. Put the knafeh pastry into a large bowl. Pull out and separate the strands and cut them into 1¼-inch | 3cm long pieces with a pair of scissors—don't worry if the pieces are uneven, it won't show in the final result. Pour over the melted butter and work it in very thoroughly with your hands, pulling out and separating the strands and turning them over, until well coated.

Spread half the pastry on the bottom of a parchment-lined 12-inch | 30cm round cake pan or 9 x 13-inch | 23 x 33cm baking dish (any shape will work) and press with the palm of your hand. Spread the ashtah over evenly (do this gently so as not to disturb the layer of pastry underneath), and cover with the rest of the pastry. Press down carefully to even out the top, and bake for about 50 minutes. Increase the temperature to 425°F, and cook for a further 10–15 minutes, until browned around the edges and golden on top.

Remove from the oven and slide a sharp knife around the edges, then leave to cool for 5 minutes. Slowly drizzle most of the sugar syrup on top and garnish with the pistachios. Serve the pie warm, with the rest of the syrup on the side.

Glossary

This glossary covers a lot of ground. My aim is to quickly and briefly inform. It does not do justice to the vast amount that can be said about these ingredients from many different perspectives.

As with all ingredients, there is a huge range in quality for each product. Price is a good guide, as you tend to get what you pay for—but more than this, buying something from a country and fair-trade supplier, such as spices, will always give you the more "authentic" (which often just translates as tastier) version of the product. Za'atar mix should have only four ingredients—dried za'atar, sumac, sesame seeds and salt—but often other ingredients are added to the mix, which don't belong there. Always read the label and ingredients list in products you buy. The best sumac, za'atar and tahini will always be found in Middle Eastern shops. However, this is not to say that shopping for everything in a supermarket or online and buying their own-brand versions is in any way wrong.

Another thing to keep in mind is that when Arabic words are translated into English, they are written phonetically. This can lead to a lot of different ways of spelling the same product: kebbeh or kubbeh, for example; hummus, hummous or hommos. I have chosen the spelling which makes more sense to use, and then stuck to it throughout.

Adha: An Arabic term meaning "pouring" or "spilling," similar to "tarka" in Indian cuisine or the Turkish kizgin tereyaği. Adha is a flavorful mixture of garlic, spices and fresh herbs heated in butter, oil or ghee and drizzled over dishes just before serving, to enhance flavor, aroma and texture. It complements a variety of dishes, including stews, soups and dips.

Akkawi cheese: A semi-hard cheese originating in Akka, a port city. Slightly salty in taste, Akkawi cheese can be consumed as is, typically for breakfast or added to salads in the same way as feta. It's also used in sweet dishes like knafeh, where its saltiness contrasts with the sweetness of sugar-syrup-drenched pastry. Before using in sweet dishes, the cheese needs to be soaked in several changes of cold water.

Aleppo chile flakes: Dried chile flakes named after the Syrian city of Aleppo, known for their medium heat and sweet aroma, similar to Turkish pul biber. These flakes can be sprinkled over various dishes, particularly enhancing the flavor of eggs, and are added to melted butter or heated oil before drizzling over stews or soups.

Baharat: Literally translating to "spices" in Arabic, baharat is a versatile spice blend with varying compositions depending on regional and household preferences. Typically, it consists of black peppercorns, coriander seeds, cinnamon, cloves, allspice, cumin, cardamom and nutmeg. It adds a sweet depth of flavor to both savory and sweet dishes.

Dibs: Dibs is an Arabic term that refers to thick, sweet molasses or syrup, most commonly made from dates, grapes and pomegranates. It is a staple ingredient in many Middle Eastern kitchens and is used in both savory and sweet dishes. Dibs is commonly drizzled over pancakes, waffles, or porridge. It can also be mixed with tahini for a quick and nutritious spread. In some Middle Eastern cuisines, dibs—for example, pomegranate molasses—are used to add depth to savory dishes, such as meat marinades or vegetable stews.

Dibs al-inab (grape molasses): This is produced by reducing grape juice until it becomes a thick syrup. It has a fruity sweetness with a slightly tangy undertone.

Dibs al-tamr (date molasses): This is made by extracting the juice from ripe dates, which is then boiled down to create a rich, thick syrup.

Dill seeds: With a scent resembling caraway and a taste reminiscent of anise, dill seeds add a spicy warmth to dishes. They pair well with acidic ingredients like lemon juice and are commonly used in Gazan cuisine, particularly in dishes like dagga, a spicy tomato salad. If unavailable, celery seeds or caraway seeds can be used as substitutes.

Egyptian rice: A type of rice similar in appearance to short-grain rice but creamier and firmer, making it suitable for long and slow-cooked dishes, or for stuffed vegetables or vine leaves. It can be substituted with other short-grain or risotto rice if necessary.

Fatteh: Fatteh means "crushed" in Arabic. It describes a type of food preparation practiced throughout the Levant, where a piece of flatbread is torn into chunks and layered into a dish. If the bread is fresh or untoasted, it will soak up the juices or sauce in a dish and collapse happily in with the other ingredients. If the pieces of bread are toasted, they will retain their shape and crunch a bit more. In this case the bread can also be used as a tool, instead of cutlery, to scoop up and eat the other ingredients in the dish.

Freekeh: Freekeh is a Middle Eastern whole grain or cracked wheat. The wheat is harvested before it is fully ripe and then roasted over an open fire so as to burn off the husks. This gives the wheat a wonderfully smoky and nutty flavor. It's widely available in well-stocked supermarkets, in specialty shops, health food shops and online.

Knafeh pastry: Popular across the Levant (as well as Turkey and Greece), knafeh or kataifi consists of long, thin strands of pastry, similar to phyllo. It's what is used to make my ashtah knafeh pie (page 302). The knafeh strands are used in various sweet or savory fillings before being baked or fried. Once the pastry is baked or fried, it takes on an enticing golden color and crispy texture, and is often drenched in a sugar syrup when used in sweet dishes. The pastry is stocked in the fresh or frozen section in Arab, Greek or Turkish grocers.

Maftoul: Also known as "Palestinian couscous" or "giant couscous," maftoul is made from sun-dried and cracked bulgur wheat rolled in flour, resulting in larger pasta-like balls. It is used to bulk up soups or stews or served with chickpeas alongside meat or fish. Fregola can be used as an alternative if maftoul is unavailable.

Mahlab: A spice with a nutty, slightly bitter almond flavor, made from grinding the kernel of the black St. Lucia cherry. It is used in bread and sweet baking, adding a unique flavor. Mahlab is also suitable for flavoring cookies, sugar syrups and whipped cream. Alternatively, a small amount of almond extract can be used as a substitute.

Mastic gum: A resin obtained from the mastic tree, primarily found on the Greek island of Chios. Mastic gum, also known as Arabic gum or Yemen gum, has a distinct flavor reminiscent of fennel, anise and mint. It is used in various dishes, such as ice cream, jams, custards and soups, to add flavor and texture. There are no direct substitutes for mastic gum.

Nabulsi cheese: Similar to Akkawi cheese, Nabulsi cheese is also a slightly salty semi-hard cheese. Traditionally made with a mix of ewe's and goat's milk in equal proportions, it is flavored with mastic, mahlab and nigella seeds. Nabulsi cheese can be used in both savory and sweet dishes.

Red pepper paste: Also known as biber salçası in Turkish, this is a common ingredient in Middle Eastern cuisine, made from chopped red peppers that are cooked down to a thick, concentrated paste consistency and used in the same way as tomato paste. There are two types of this paste on the market, spicy and mild.

Sumac: A tangy spice made from grinding dried sumac berries, commonly used in Palestinian cooking to season dishes such as roasted vegetables, meat, fish or eggs. It can also be added to slow-cooked onions for traditional dishes like chicken musahkhan.

Tahini: A paste made from ground sesame seeds, tahini is creamy, nutty and pourable, and is commonly used in Middle Eastern cuisine. It can be drizzled over roasted vegetables, fish or meat, or spread on toast or spooned over ice cream. Creamy Lebanese and Palestinian brands are preferred over Greek or Cypriot ones as I find them smoother and easier to cook with.

Za'atar: Refers to both a wild herb, a variety of oregano, and a spice mix commonly used in Palestinian cuisine. The spice mix includes dried za'atar, toasted sesame seeds, sumac and salt. It has a savory aroma with complex flavors reminiscent of oregano, marjoram, cumin, lemon, sage and mint. Za'atar is versatile and is used to season dishes like eggs, salads, grilled meat or fish, or served with olive oil as a dip for bread.

Index

About the author

Sami Tamimi is a Palestinian chef, restaurateur and food writer who is based between London, UK, and Umbria, Italy. Sami grew up in the old city of Jerusalem, before leaving on a journey of self-discovery, first to Tel Aviv and then to London.

With more than thirty-five years of experience, Sami's fascination with food, which later turned into an obsession, began at an early age in his mum's kitchen. His professional cooking career began at seventeen, working as a porter at the Mount Zion Hotel in Jerusalem, where he quickly became a chef in charge of breakfast. From there he went on to work in different restaurants, cafés and even a hospital kitchen to gain experience and learn as much as possible about food.

At twenty-one, Sami moved to Tel Aviv where he set up a small catering business and continued to work in restaurants, leading to a position at Lilith, one of the most renowned restaurants in Israel at the time. Working his way up, he became head chef at Lilith where he spent five years working with Karen Handler-Kremmerman, whom he considers his mentor.

After moving to London in 1997, Sami ran the savory kitchen at Baker & Spice. At this food and bakery shop in Chelsea, he was given the freedom to show his talent and creativity in the deli side of the business, which later turned into a successful catering business, putting Baker & Spice on the foodie map of London. The company preserved Sami's legacy and expanded to different locations in London and other parts of the world.

In 2002, Sami partnered with Yotam Ottolenghi (whom he met and worked with at Baker & Spice) and Noam Bar to open the first Ottolenghi deli in Notting Hill. The company has since expanded to more locations in London, including five delis and two restaurants: NOPI and ROVI.

At Ottolenghi, Sami and Yotam created a concept that has proven a huge success from day one, serving trademark savory foods and pastries, providing catering and running two busy restaurants in central London. Over the years, Sami was in charge of food creativity and nurturing younger chefs around the company.

Sami and Yotam have written two critically acclaimed cookbooks, *Ottolenghi* and *Jerusalem*, the latter winning many awards, including the International Book Award from the James Beard Foundation in 2013. *Jerusalem* has been credited with starting many cookbook clubs all over the world.

Sami's third cookbook *Falastin* is co-authored with Tara Wigley and was the winner of the Fortnum & Mason Cookery Book of the Year 2021, James Beard Award Nominee 2022, IACP Award winner and Longlisted for The Art Of Eating Prize 2021.

Acknowledgments

My biggest acknowledgment and thanks go to my parents, Hassan and Na'ama, for always inspiring my cooking.

Thanks to Tamara Gillon and Zahra Saaidi for cooking the recipes with me.

Big gratitude to Basia Murphy for your friendship and for the huge part you took on yourself in reading all the text of this book before it went to my publishers.

Thanks to Jeremy for his support and for putting up with me for the last twenty years, and for always being happy to eat my repetitive creations.

Thanks also to the Tamimi clan, Sawsan, Kawthar, Olla, Adel, Adnan and Azam. Love you all.

As always, I am totally grateful to Jane Finigan and Felicity Rubinstein.

Huge thank you to the team at Ebury: Liv Nightingall, Steph Milner, Joel Rickett, Celia Palazzo, Stephenie Reynolds, Lara McLeod, Anjali Nathani and Lizzy Gray.

Thanks also to Kim Witherspoon and to the team in North America: Aaron Wehner, Katherine Tyler, Molly Birnbaum, Afton Cyrus and Robert McCullough.

For the design and look of the book, thanks to Claire Rochford. Photography, huge thanks to Ola Ostaszewska Smit and Issy Croker: I was so lucky to have you both as my food photographers, and thanks to Martyna Wlodarsk for assisting. For props, thanks to Wei Tang, Charlie Phillips and Louie Waller. For editing and proofreading, thanks to Annie Lee and Imogen Fortes.

Full respect also to Rafaella, Ianthe, Frances and the rest of team at TONIC STUDIO.

To Pierre Malouf and Noor Murad for your friendship and the funny sense of humor.

Special thank you to Helen Goh, Tali Levin, Eric Rodari and Wei Tang.

Thanks to MaryAnn Jaraisy for your friendship and support. Thanks to Umayya and Samia Abu Hanna and the rest of the Hummus Academy team.

Special thank you to the Kelly Penny family, George, Maureen, Georgina, Louis and Darren.

Thanks to Gianluca Piermaria and his family for having me as part of the family and for feeding me all their delicious Italian food.

A big thank you to my friend Dr. Ramzi Khamis and his family.

Thanks, Alejandra Chavero: you are more than family to me. Also, big thank you to your dear mum, Maria, for caring and inspiring.

Thanks to Reg and Bea, aka Bobo and Bibi, for bringing so much joy into our lives.

Tᴇɴ Sᴘᴇᴇᴅ Pʀᴇss
An imprint of the Crown Publishing Group
A division of Penguin Random House LLC
1745 Broadway
New York, NY 10019
tenspeed.com
penguinrandomhouse.com

Originally published in the United Kingdom by Ebury Press, an imprint
of Ebury Publishing, a division of Penguin Random House UK.

Typefaces: Latinotype's Campeche and Monotype's Fnord

Library of Congress Cataloging-in-Publication Data
Names: Tamimi, Sami, author.
Title: Boustany : vegan and vegetarian recipes from Palestine / Sami Tamimi.
Identifiers: LCCN 2024054155 (print) | LCCN 2024054156 (ebook) | ISBN
9781984863188 (hardcover) | ISBN 9781984863195 (ebook)
Subjects: LCSH: Cooking, Palestinian Arab. | Vegetarian cooking—Palestine. |
LCGFT: Cookbooks.
Classification: LCC TX725.P237 T36 2025 (print) | LCC TX725.P237 (ebook) |
DDC 641.5/636095694—dc23/eng/20241205
LC record available at https://lccn.loc.gov/2024054155
LC ebook record available at https://lccn.loc.gov/2024054156

Hardcover ISBN 978-1-9848-6318-8
Ebook ISBN 978-1-9848-6319-5

Editor: Molly Birnbaum | Production editor: Terry Deal
Editorial assistant: Gabby Ureña Matos
Designer: Claire Rochford | Co-designer: Kelly Booth
Production designer: Mari Gill
Production: Jane Chinn
Food stylist: Tamara Gillon, Lara Cook, and Noor Murad
Prop stylist: Louie Waller, Charlie Phillips, and Wei Tang
Photo assistant: Martyna Wlodarska
Americanizer: Afton Cyrus | Proofreader: Rebecca Zaharia
Publicist: David Hawk | Marketer: Monica Stanton

Manufactured in China

10 9 8 7 6 5 4 3 2 1

First US Edition

The authorized representative in the EU for product safety and compliance
is Penguin Random House Ireland, Morrison Chambers, 32 Nassau Street,
Dublin D02 YH68, Ireland, https://eu-contact.penguin.ie.